Erasmus Kloman

bare barging in burgundy

BOATING, EXPLORING, WINING & DINING

Erasmus Kloman

bare barging in
burgundy

BOATING, EXPLORING, WINING & DINING

CAPITAL
BOOKS, INC.

Capital Books, Inc.
P.O. Box 605
Herndon, Virginia 20172-0605

Library of Congress Cataloging-in-Publication Data

Kloman, Erasmus H.
  Bare barging in Burgundy : boating, exploring, wining & dining /
Erasmus H. Kloman.
    p. cm.
  ISBN 1-892123-40-1   (alk. paper)
    1. Burgundy (France)—Description and travel. 2. Burgundy (France)—
History. 3. Kloman, Erasmus H.—Journeys—France—Burgundy.
4. Barges—France—Burgundy. 5. Cookery, French—Burgundy style.
6. Wine and wine making—France—Burgundy. I. Title.
DC611.B773 K56 2001
914.4′410484—dc21   00-054726

Printed in the United States of America on acid-free paper that meets the American National Standards Institute Z39-48 Standard.

First Edition

10 9 8 7 6 5 4 3 2 1

On the cover: The Port of Auxerre. Detail of a painting by Erasmus Kloman.

TABLE OF CONTENTS

ACKNOWLEDGMENTS

The idea for this book began to take shape well before our family barge trip in June 1999. In preparation for the trip I had begun collecting background materials including books and articles concerning everything for which Burgundy is noted, starting with the network of waterways for barging, but also including the region's history, its cuisines, and its world-renowned wines. Thus, I should first acknowledge my great debt to the many authorities on Burgundy who plowed the ground before me and facilitated my research enormously. Their names and the titles of their books appear in the bibliography, a chapter-by-chapter listing of my sources and, I hope, a useful curriculum for readers contemplating a barge trip. Such advance reading contributes beyond measure to the pleasures of this form of travel. Internet surfers will find as I did a wealth of information in the sites listed in the Internet Appendix.

Many friends and associates provided invaluable assistance by reading and commenting on the manuscript in its several drafts. First, I want to express my gratitude to the late Eve Jaffe of the Travel Books and Language Center in Washington, D.C., who encouraged me and gave helpful tips when I was starting a book proposal. Patricia Hass, who has counseled me on both of my earlier books on France, again provided her expert knowledge at the start of the project. The late Burke Wilkinson, author of *Francis in All His Glory,* helped me sort out some of the convolutions of French history. Anna Fierst, who with her husband, David, knows Burgundy and barging from first-hand experience, critiqued and edited the manuscript at several stages. Howard Dougherty, The Barge Broker, from whom we chartered our barge, reviewed the manuscript with special attention to the chapter on our week's cruise, the centerpiece of the book. The appendix on wines was reviewed by Joe Kluchinsky of MacArthur Beverages, one of Washington's most knowledgeable wine authorities. My grateful thanks go also to Jackie Rush, the trusty agent who has helped with all our travels in France, and to Monica Hammock, my computer consultant.

My thanks to the French Government Tourist Office and the Eastern France Tourist Board, which provided the list of charter companies in Appendix B. I am also indebted to the restaurants that provided favorite recipes for reproduction in the text: La Grande Chaumière in St.-Floren-tin, Barnabet in Auxerre, and L'Etape des Gourmets in Chatel-Censoir.

The book would never have happened without the understanding and assistance of my wife, Suzanne. Her daily diary faithfully recording life on board our barge, the *Matisse*, was the skeleton on which I based the narrative of the cruise. Equally essential were her meticulous editing of the manuscript and her insistence on clarifying and simplifying my prolix prose.

Sue's daughter Nancy, her husband, Tom, and their three daughters joined us on the *Matisse* and were ideal companions, helping to bring about the many rewards that such an adventure promises. We thank them all for their company, especially Tom in his roles of cool-headed skipper and reviewer of parts of my manuscript.

Credit for final editing at Capital Books goes with my great apprecia-tion to Jeanne Hickman. Working with my publisher, Kathleen Hughes, has been the kind of experience that every author hopes for.

Try as I might to find ways to spread the blame for any errors or imperfections in this book, I cannot escape from assuming full responsi-bility for the final product.

PREFACE

The popularity of barge trips in France and elsewhere in Europe has been growing rapidly in recent years. In France alone, more than 200,000 people enjoy this pastime each year on a fleet of approximately 55,000 inland waterway vessels. Whether on the less expensive and more adventuresome bare barges or the more luxurious hotel barges (with amenities closer to that of hotels), tourists are discovering the great appeal of this kind of vacation. So far this appeal has almost totally escaped the French themselves, but it has triggered an enthusiastic response among English and other European tourists and among more and more Americans seeking new ways to experience France. A similar phenomenon has taken place on the canals and rivers of neighboring countries, especially Germany, Belgium, and the Netherlands, as well as England.

In June 1999 my wife, Sue, and I had our third barge trip in France, this one being a bare (or self-drive) barge starting on the Burgundy canal. With us were my wife's elder daughter Nancy, her husband, Tom, and our three granddaughters, Kate, Perrin, and Julia, ranging in age from ten to seventeen. Tom, an experienced mariner, served as skipper, with the rest of us as crew. We all have spent a good deal of time on boats, but such prior experience, though helpful, is not a prerequisite for a barge cruise. With Tom at the helm much but not all of the time, we navigated our seven-day cruise in the allotted time, while enjoying a leisurely passage through the beautiful unspoiled countryside of provincial France. Measured by any standard, the trip was a huge success.

Sue's and my two previous barge trips were in hotel barges. As their name suggests, such barges resemble floating hotels with the amenities, staff, and higher prices associated with hotels. Our first trip, in 1984, was on the Burgundy canal with two other couples, and the second, in 1996, on the Canal Lateral à La Garonne with one other couple. These two memorable experiences had encouraged us to invite Sue's daughter and her family to join us on the Burgundy canal trip. Originally they were in favor of a hotel barge, but we convinced them that the bare barge would be more informal and more fun for the girls. Everyone now agrees that we made the right choice. Son-in-law Tom enjoyed

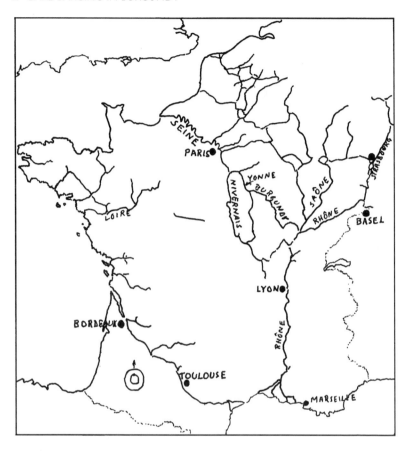

the challenge of guiding our barge, the *Matisse*, along the waterways; the granddaughters enjoyed handling the lines and helping to maneuver the sixty-seven locks on our route; and my wife and her daughter enjoyed their not-too-demanding culinary roles, shopping for breakfast and picnic lunch on board and selecting the most promising restaurants for dinner in the small villages where we tied up for the night. Best of all was the rare opportunity to spend unhurried time in conversation, allowing our three generations to get inside each other's heads.

The format of this book follows that of my two earlier books on France, *Sojourn in Gascony: Pleasures of the Palette,* published in 1994, and *Apartment in Paris: Renting, Roaming, Wining, and Dining,* published in 1998. Just as the two earlier books are a mixture of the romance of travel in France and the practical how-to questions facing renters of French houses or apartments, so this book aspires to fit in the literary travel genre. It is aimed at a diverse readership—not only those contemplating a barge trip but also those who may enjoy vicariously the experience of a leisurely passage through the storied French countryside of Burgundy. The remarkable history, the magnificent architecture, and the hearty cuisine of this ancient land have scarcely received the attention they merit in travel literature. The day-to-day account of our trip in chapter 2 is the centerpiece of the book and will be of primary interest to readers wanting to learn about the practical and recreational aspects of barging. Readers with primary interests in history, cooking, or wines may wish to focus on those subjects. Burgundy is great country for biking or walking, and this book may be useful to landlubbers as well as bargers. A series of appendices covers sources of information on barge charter companies, Internet information sources, recipes, and restaurants. An annotated bibliography lists publications on barging and related topics.

This book seeks to add a personal dimension to much of the literature on barging. I hope that readers will be able to visualize the experience as seen through my eyes, so that they are in effect taking the trip with our family on board the *Matisse*. For those who wonder what the lure of barging is all about, I hope this book will provide an answer.

Erasmus H. Kloman
Washington, D.C.
on the web at www.Klomantravelbooks.com

INTRODUCTION
PLANNING

"Believe me, my young friend, there is nothing—absolutely nothing—half so much worth doing as simply messing about in boats."
Water Rat to Mole in Kenneth Grahame's *Wind in the Willows*

Rat said it all when he uttered this memorable pronouncement. Boating has long enjoyed universal acceptance whether on the willow-lined banks of the Thames from Cookham to Pangbourne in England, across the channel in French waterways, or wherever in the world the joys of this pastime are known. Rat went on to say about boats: "In or out of 'em, it doesn't matter. Nothing seems really to matter, that's the charm of it. Whether you get away, or whether you don't; whether you arrive at your destination or whether you reach somewhere else, or whether you never get anywhere at all, you're always busy, and you never do anything in particular."

Although once afloat on a barge on the French waterways, one should expect the same kind of lackadaisical pleasures enjoyed by Rat, organizing a barge trip is somewhat more complicated. Rat's boating excursions were pretty spontaneous affairs. When he decided to go out on the river, he'd go into his kitchen and instantly emerge with a wicker luncheon basket laden with all the makings of a picnic feast. No preparations, no planning needed! But with a barge trip some planning is necessary: it is part of the adventure and should definitely be part of the fun. Collecting all the information you need to decide where, when, and how to go barging should be a rewarding and enjoyable exercise in anticipation. The more time and consideration you invest in this exercise, the more you will, like Rat and Mole, enjoy your time afloat. And even if you decide not to go, the learning experience and its vicarious pleasures should be sufficient reward. My hope is that even readers not planning a barge trip may find here adventures of the mind while learning about the history of Burgundy and its many attractions.

What Area of France? Not an Easy Choice

The map of the canals and navigable waterways shows how many choices there are in France alone, to say nothing of all the barging possibilities in other countries. Since France has the most extensive and well-developed canal network, this book deals only with the French system and focuses especially on one of the most popular barging regions, Burgundy. However, selecting an area in France is anything but easy, for there are many alluring and picturesque areas of countryside to choose from. As the French say about an embarrassment of riches, *"Les choix ne manquent pas."* Each prospective barger will have personal preferences based on such variables as past travel in France, timing of vacation, and budgetary constraints.

As for the trip on which this book is based, my wife and I enjoyed a special luxury not available to everyone. We started planning the trip nearly two years before the event and greatly enjoyed an advance scouting expedition of potential barge routes in 1998. Anyone who can find the time should do a scouting trip just for the fun of it. Ours took place after we had found that Sue's daughter and her family were already planning to go to France in 1999 and were delighted at the prospect of a barge trip to precede their week in Paris.

A Scouting Mission in Alsace

Our 1998 scouting mission took us east from Paris by train to Alsace, an area of France bordering on the Rhine, which we had not visited before. It was easy to see how the distinctive qualities of this area, influenced as it is by its German and Swiss neighbors, have struck a responsive chord with tourists. The Saône River with its rural landscapes set against a background of dark forests is one of the most beautiful French waterways, and the canal system linking such cities as Strasbourg, Colmar, and Mulhouse have to be high on a list of desirable areas for barging.

Strasbourg served as our base for exploring this area. After two days walking around the city, observing its canals by tour boats, and checking out the marinas and barge facilities, we realized that we had only scratched the surface of this fascinating city. But we also wanted to explore the environs, and thus rented a car for day trips.

A powerful argument can be made for selecting a barge route that includes Strasbourg, just to be able to spend some time there. Begun as a Roman trading center, the city became a medieval crossroads and still serves as a vital pathway between east and west. Its thirteenth-century Cathedral of Notre-Dame, forming the nucleus of the old town, is encircled by mostly pedestrian streets. Strasbourg is a pedestrian's paradise because nearly all historic sites are on streets closed to motor vehicles. Our hotel, the Hôtel de Rohan, was conveniently located on one of these cobblestone streets within a stone's throw of the cathedral. One of the city's most enchanting areas is La Petite France, a section of ancient half-timbered buildings lining both sides of the River Ill where tanners once carried on their trade.

Interesting tidbits of Strasbourg history include the facts that Johann Gutenberg started out in the printing trade here; the French national anthem, *la Marseillaise,* was written here; and Marie Antoinette married Louis XVI here. Strasbourg has considerable stature in contemporary political and economic affairs as the home of the Parliament of Europe.

Sovereignty over Alsace–Lorraine, the most fought-over area in all of western Europe, has been bitterly contested by France and Germany, and the territory has shifted from one to another four times in the last two centuries. A part of France since the end of World War II, it still is a delicious *mélange* of the two cultures as reflected in architecture, place names, and cuisine.

Culinary Considerations

The Michelin Guide, which awards three stars to only fifteen restaurants outside of Paris in all of France, gives this honor to three restaurants in or near Strasbourg. Since Sue is a serious cook and we appreciate fine cuisine, we were impressed by this cluster of stars. But we do not consider ourselves food snobs. While we respect the serious nature of the Michelin and the several other culinary ranking systems, we are not bound to them. We find many restaurants with no stars much to our liking, and are almost always happy when dining in one- or two-star restaurants. It is interesting to see places seeking to add stars. Our visits to three-star restaurants are fairly infrequent. But several friends had urged us to go to the Auberge de l'Ill between Strasbourg and Colmar, where we enjoyed a memorable luncheon in a beautiful setting. (See Appendix E for discussion of restaurant rankings.)

Nothing ranks much higher than cuisine in our weighing of alternative destinations for travel. Since my wife is such a dedicated cook and has taught me to appreciate good cooking, we pay a lot of attention to restaurants and culinary styles when contemplating travel. We followed this course in Alsace. Stemming from its mixed cultural heritage, Alsatian cooking combines the robust earthiness of German fare with the greater sophistication of French cuisine. The area boasts a superabundance of good restaurants with each type of cooking, and many restaurant menus offer both styles of cuisine. But hearty German fare with heaping dishes of *choucroute,* pork and other types of sausages, *pot-au-feu,* and potatoes is the cuisine for which Alsace is best known. With my German heritage and a palate accommodating different cuisines, I was more disposed to accept the German dishes than Sue who strongly favors French and Italian cooking.

We much enjoyed the famous Alsatian wines, especially the Rieslings and the Gewurztraminers. Although restaurant menus offered many traditional wines from other regions of France, it seemed foolish not to savor the products of local vineyards. The Alsatian wine region ranks third in all of France, trailing only Bordeaux and Burgundy. Almost all are white, mostly fruity and fresh, and, with their clean-tasting quality,

well suited to accompany the often heavy Alsatian cuisine. These wines, unlike other French whites, are good companions to red meat. Now, back in the States, we choose Alsatian wines from time to time in restaurants or for home consumption.

Southwest into Burgundy: Beaune and Dijon

Our scouting itinerary called for checking out the canals and barge facilities in Alsace and then driving southwest into Burgundy. Rive de France, the barge company we were considering for our charter, had given us maps showing sites of their marinas. On the way to our lunch at l'Auberge de l'Ill, we visited the Rive de France marina at Krafft, just below Strasbourg. Although in mid-October the facility was closed, we could judge what it had to offer in the way of fuel, water, and other necessities.

The next major stop on our itinerary was Beaune, our base for exploring canal networks in the lower part of Burgundy. Until the fourteenth century, Beaune was the residence of the Dukes of Burgundy before they moved to Dijon. It lies at the center of the famed Burgundian

vineyards, and much of its thriving economy is based on wine. We stayed in the highly recommended Hôtel de la Poste, a small luxury hotel built originally as a postal relay stop. Recently it received high marks from the discriminating newsletter *La Belle France*. Having visited Beaune several years before and toured its famous Hôtel-Dieu, we decided to focus on other sites, including the Burgundy Wine Museum in the restored palace of the Dukes of Burgundy, a fifteenth to sixteenth-century mansion. The fourteenth-century wine cellar behind an enormous door displays wine presses and vats, while the ground floor presents the history of Burgundian viniculture from Roman times.

On our visit to the marina facilities in Dijon, we found quite a few large hotel barges mothballed for the winter months as well as smaller pleasure boats, only two of which had owners aboard. In October the quayside was relatively quiet except for a game of *boules* (or *pétanque*). As with *boules* all over France, the players were totally absorbed in their game, though this one was less disputatious than others we have

witnessed. The absence of commotion added to an end-of-season languor at the dockside. During the season, however, the Dijon port is the principal hub for hotel barges that take passengers on gastronomical/cultural tours in all directions from this center. Dijon's population of some 140,000 is seven times that of Beaune, and the town's historical importance shows in the wide range of architectural and cultural sites to visit. It is the largest city on the Burgundy Canal, which runs from St. Mammes southeast of Paris to St. Jean-de-Losnes, southeast of Dijon. The latter's Office of Tourism touts it as "the premier river sailing port of France."

Auxerre and Montbard

The following day we visited two important barging towns, Montbard on the Burgundy Canal and Auxerre on the Nivernais, which connects with the Burgundy. In 1984 Sue and I had taken our first barge trip starting in Auxerre and winding up in Montbard. Montbard has a number of interesting sites to visit but nowhere near what Auxerre has to offer. This ancient capital of lower Burgundy had impressed us so favorably that we had revisited it by car several years later. In thinking about a route for another barge trip, we were strongly disposed to return to Auxerre one more time.

At about this point we began weighing the merits of Burgundy versus Alsace, a very hard choice. As an introduction to France, we thought that Burgundy might give our granddaughters a more representative impression. Other factors in its favor were its central geographic location and its historic place in French history. Our preference for classic French cuisine and the Burgundian wines pointed us in the same direction. You may wonder if our taste buds really led to our choice, and who can tell how we would have fared if we had chosen Alsace? But in hindsight we feel this was the best way to go for our group.

Bare Barge versus Hotel Barge

Our next major choices were the type of barge and the charter company. Whether to go for a self-drive or a hotel barge with a crew was the first issue. Since Sue and I had already been on two hotel barges, we were inclined to opt for a self-drive on this outing. Sue's daughter was a bit skeptical at first, fearing that shopping and cooking would make the trip more like real life than vacation. She wondered if the additional costs involved in a hotel barge trip weren't justified by the ease and comfort of life on board. We argued that the granddaughters might find the slow pace of progress on the water pretty boring and that the line-handling tasks involved in taking a bare barge through the locks would give them something to do and a sense of accomplishment.

Our argument prevailed, and it soon became apparent that we had made the right decision. Providing breakfast and lunch on board called for shopping in local food shops—far more fun than a burden. And seeking out restaurants for dinner in the towns along our route gave us an excuse for daily explorations into the countryside. Hotel barge chefs turn out Cordon Bleu dishes from their tiny galleys, but their passengers miss out on the local color in village shops and markets and the small restaurants along the route of the cruise.

Opting for the bare barge, however, involves a tradeoff. Shopping and food preparation for two meals each day on board require time. One should not expect the same kind of elaborate picnic lunch in a wicker basket that mysteriously materializes in Water Rat's kitchen to emerge from the galley of a bare barge. Without such miracle repasts, there was less time than we might have wanted for side trips to historic sites. A hotel barge, accompanied by a car or van to take guests on daily outings, provides access to sites some distance from the canal and to restaurants that may outclass those in the small villages near the water-ways. In our case, with the exception of one dreadful meal, we found the local restaurants entirely satisfactory. However, connoisseurs seeking gourmet dining and wining experiences and prepared to pay the addi-tional premiums might prefer the hotel barge.

It's Easy to Be Your Own Captain

As noted above, prior boating experience, though helpful, is not a prerequisite for barging. Anyone can drive a barge who uses care and common sense, but the prospective barger should be prepared to cope with a variety of situations, none of them particularly daunting and all made less challenging by some basic familiarity with boats. Charter companies provide charts of the route and brief you on the operation of the boat before you take off. A barge company mechanic is never more than a phone call away. Son-in-law Tom, an experienced and cool-headed mariner, was ideally suited (really overqualified) to be the skipper of the *Matisse*. While one incident discussed in chapter 2 called for a skilled machinist's ingenuity and almost superhuman fortitude, the rest of the trip went smoothly. There was, however, the daily adventure of passing through an average of eight locks in order to make our final destination on schedule. In selecting a route for your trip, you should take account of the distance to be covered, the number of locks, and the amount of barge traffic you are likely to encounter. If you opt, as we did, for a one-way route rather than a roundtrip, you must pace your progress so as to deliver your barge to the final destination at a specified time. A roundtrip route allows greater flexibility. You can go only as far on the way out as you choose, lolling around wherever and whenever you like, provided you return the barge to your point of departure. Of course, the downside is that you see less of the countryside by doubling back.

Choosing a Barge Company

The list of sixteen barge companies in Appendix B, maintained by the eastern France Tourist Board, indicates the extent of popular interest in barging. Practically every year new companies are entering this flourishing market. They all provide illustrated literature showing the various models of their barges, charts and photographs of the waterways they cover, and price lists. Obviously, the more information you gather from these companies, the better equipped you will be to make informed choices.

We relied on our Washington travel agent to suggest a barge broker. Though he was in the rather unlikely location of Boulder, Colorado, bare barges in France were one of his specialties, and he represented most of the major companies offering this kind of service. Over 500 barges are registered in the fleets of his companies. He also represents various hotel barge companies.

Hotel barges vary in size and number of guests accommodated. The first barge trip Sue and I made on the Burgundy canal, in 1984, had room for three couples plus the crew, and the other two couples were old friends. We all share fond memories of that barging experience. On our second trip, in 1995, we traveled along the Canal Lateral à la Garonne on a barge skippered by an American, Kate Ratliffe, who doubled as a gourmet chef. It could take only four guests, and again our companions were friends of long standing.

It is preferable to be with friends when spending a week in close quarters on a barge. However, many of the hotel barges take large groups. Just as you face questions about fellow travelers when you sign up for a seagoing cruise, so you may wonder how other guests aboard a hotel barge will be as traveling companions.

Some people deal with this situation by lining up friends or relatives to join them, thus assuring good company. We know of one couple who signed up for what sounded like a wonderful hotel barge trip. After an initial hitch which delayed the departure of the barge, the couple went on board and found that all the other guests had come as a group, and quite a rowdy group at that. The couple was so put off that they left the barge and happily spent the rest of the week in Paris.

Companions for a barge trip should be people who would be easy to get along with in close quarters, either adventuresome enough to explore the countryside on foot or bikes, or content just to watch the scenery pass by and willing to banter a bit with the lockkeepers in French. Never mind if your French is fractured, the lockkeepers appreciate any efforts to communicate in their language. It's customary to tip them several francs (the going rate is now about five francs) as you pass through the lock. On our trip Julia, the youngest granddaughter, was delegated to hand over the tips, and she was always greeted warmly by whoever was operating the lock. All three granddaughters used their school-taught French in encounters with locals we met along the way and honed their language skills in the process.

Most of the other bargers we encountered were English-speaking, but there were several groups of French speakers with whom we chatted casually either when going through the locks or tied up at marinas. Like boat people worldwide, the other bargers were salt-of-the-earth types willing to lend a hand with line-handling or any other nautical situation.

Some Practical Tips

Because of the growing popularity of barging, charter companies may become booked up as much as a year in advance of the next barging season. Be prepared to reserve early. In the case of bare barges, most companies try to make the logistics of picking up and surrendering the barge as accommodating as possible. If you arrive at your barge by car, they will arrange to deliver you from your drop-off destination back to your car at the end of your trip. If you travel by train to the closest station to your barge, there will either be a car to meet you or you will have to take a taxi. Bare bargers should allow plenty of time before the actual departure for barge operating instructions and purchasing supplies. The companies provide a list of all items furnished with the charter, and they check to see that these are on board before you leave the boat.

For Americans not fluent in French it makes sense to choose a charter company based in the United States or England. Some basic knowledge of French is a real plus, if not absolutely essential, for bare barging since few lockkeepers speak English. On shore your French, even if primitive, will help you find your way around.

Whether you choose a hotel or a bare barge, you should travel light. Stowage capacity is limited, especially on bare barges, and you should plan to dress mainly for comfort. Take sneakers or topsiders, quick-dry clothes, and marine-type foul-weather gear. Confine your baggage as much as possible to canvas duffles that can be stowed away in small spaces.

Bicycles are a big part of the fun of barging. Some charter companies include them as part of the charter costs; others charge extra for them on request of the customer. But sometimes the bikes are not in good shape, and it is very important to test each of them before embarking. Some serious bikers go to the trouble of taking their own bikes along and may use them for biking before or after their cruise. Taking a spare inner tube on board in case of a flat is a good idea.

On the waterways you will probably pass fishermen whose rods extend well out into the waterway. Do not expect them to pull their lines in for your passage. Slow down your engine, wave to them, and wish them *Bonne chance*. These fisher folk and boat people have different perspectives on how the canals should be enjoyed.

When tying up along the banks of a canal, watch out for any obstruction that may hinder your departure when you're ready to leave. Watch out for the tall grass under water that can wrap around your propeller.

The best times of year for barging are the spring and early summer months of April, May, and June. Later in July and August the waterways and on-shore marina facilities are likely to be more crowded by other vacationers. Locks may be closed for weather conditions (flooding in March and drought in September) or repairs in the offseason.

Costs

The costs of a barge vacation depend on many variables: the size of the barge; the season (high season versus offseason); the waterway route; and most important, the choice between a hotel barge and a bare barge. The relatively luxurious lifestyle on hotel barges drives up the per person costs in comparison with the do-it-yourself lifestyle of the bare barges. Even on the latter, costs depend on such questions as whether you cook all meals on board or dine out at restaurants along your route. The charter companies listed in Appendix B offer a wide variety of barging options, and comparison shopping is the best way to find what suits your travel goals and your budget.

The easiest way to compare costs is to check the Internet sources listed in Appendix C, with sites not only for Burgundy but in France and elsewhere in Europe as well. The Burgundy canal site, for example, presents a table comparing costs for four major bare boat charter companies and three separate lists comparing hotel barges by various measures.

The price of our week's charter was about $4,000 which did not include travel to and from the barge marina, food and drinks, restaurant meals, and incidentals. On a per person basis, that breaks down to about $560 for our group—very reasonable for a week's travel anywhere on earth. To take seven people on a hotel barge, the total costs would range from about $12,000 to $30,000 or more depending on some of the variables cited above. Hotel barges normally include transfers to and from the barge, Cordon Bleu cuisine, full open bar, escorted excursions, and admissions to the various sites visited. Basically, everything but the gratuity for the crew is included. All cabins have private facilities.

Public telephones are available in the towns and villages along your route, but it can be a great convenience to have your own cellular phone as a link to the outside world. Be aware that U.S. phones do not work in Europe, and you must take one designed for overseas communication. We did not have such a phone on our trip in 1999 and only discovered the great value of such a gadget during our travels the following year.

Information Sources

The bibliography covers books on barging, the history of Burgundy, its cuisines, and its wines. You can learn a great deal about the history of this area through guidebooks, especially the green Michelin. Be sure to take a guidebook along with you. The barge companies all provide promotional literature on the regions where they operate as well as the various types of charters they offer. The French Government Tourist Office with branches in New York, Chicago, and Los Angeles has a wealth of literature for potential bargers. All the major search engines of the Internet provide barging information in their travel sections, and major barge companies including Rive de France have web pages. (See Appendix C.)

Whatever type of barge you choose and whatever waterways you travel, your pleasure will be greatly enhanced if you invest time in planning your adventure, comparing the numerous offerings of charters to select the one best suited to your needs, recruiting friends or family members to share the joys of your journey, and reading about the history of the land you are traversing.

ONE 🍇
Some Glimpses of the Past

The Concept of Burgundy

Most people who know France are familiar with the name of Burgundy and think of it as one of the regions now famous for its wines. Not so many are aware of Burgundy's unique place in French history or how close Burgundy came to displacing France as the supreme power. Though it is hard to imagine that the nation we call France might have been called Burgundy with Dijon as capital rather than Paris, the lands under Burgundy's dominion far exceeded the territory of France and actually held France in a kind of vise. Only with the battlefield death of the last of the four great dukes of Burgundy in 1477 did it come under French dominion. At another stage, Burgundy came close to being absorbed into the Holy Roman Empire. Today, since Burgundy survived as just one of the regions of France rather than its political center, we can be thankful that its beautiful unspoiled landscape was not turned into a sprawling megalopolis like that surrounding Paris.

To grasp the history of this enchanted land, we must go back a long way, because what we now call Burgundy has always been a crossroads between the Paris basin and the Mediterranean south. Human habitation dates back to 18,000 B.C.E. During the Roman era the decisive battle for the whole of Gaul, in which Caesar conquered the forces led by the celebrated Vercingetorix (whose exploits still resound in Asterix comic books), was fought at Alesia, not far from Dijon. In the present-day town of Alise-Ste.-Reine, a statue of Vercingetorix commemorates his army's noble but vain attempt to withstand the Roman siege. After surrendering to the Romans, this noble warrior gave himself up in exchange for a pledge that all his men would be freed. Then, after suffering for six harsh years in a Roman prison, he died at the hands of his captors who strangled him. Although two other sites have claimed to be the actual location of this historic battle, excavations carried out

1

by Napoleon III in the 1860s substantially authenticated the claim of Alise-Ste.-Reine.

The Early Christian Era

History buffs will recall that the Gallic wars ended in 51 B.C.E. Afterwards, Roman civilization spread, and in 313 Emperor Constantine granted freedom of worship to Christians. Christianity slowly began to permeate the area which would come to be called Burgundy. That name did not come into use until the fifth century when the Saône plain was settled by a barbarian tribe that migrated all the way from the Baltic coast. This tribe, more culturally advanced than other Frankish invaders, named their new land after their old homeland, Burgundia. But other more warlike Franks seized the territory and absorbed it into their dominion. Only with the death of Charlemagne in 814 and the subsequent division of his empire did the old Burgundy, allotted to the rule of Charles the Bald, spring back to a life of its own. The duchy of

Burgundy along the right bank of the Saône was born. This region known now principally for its vineyards has a many-faceted past replete with some surprising and little-known events. In this brief synopsis we will touch only on some of the critical turning points and major figures.

The Monastic Orders

In the Middle Ages, Burgundy attained considerable prominence as the main base of the two major monastic orders, the Benedictines and the Cistercians. Monasteries of each order, some in ruins and others beautifully restored, are still dominant features of the Burgundian landscape. Sue and I have visited many of these monasteries, and we believe that any visitor to Burgundy should see at least a sampling of them. We admit to a strong preference for the simplicity and austerity of the Cistercian architectural style.

Under the strict regime of St. Bernard, founder of the Cistercian order, this style evolved as the purest structural form, its simplicity and lack of distracting adornment assuring maximum concentration of the faithful on worship. The rules of architectural style applied not only to the church but to all buildings in the monastery complex.

St. Bernard influenced not only the life of the church but the entire world in which he moved. Born to a noble family whose Château de Fontaine was located near Dijon, he renounced all his inheritance at the age of twenty-one and, with a group of companions, went to the monastery of Citeaux in search of God's mercy. His leadership qualities came almost instantly to the fore, as he rose to the position of abbot and instituted reforms which turned the troubled body of the faithful he had found into one of the most illustrious monasteries of the age. Bernard was passionate almost to the point of violence in his belief that the main body of the Church, as represented chiefly by the Benedictine order, had gone in the wrong direction, especially in its striving for architectural grandeur and worldly splendor. He railed against the excessive size of contemporary cathedrals and the sumptuous ornaments that distract the eyes of worshipers. He found these massive structures too big, too ostentatious, and too distant from his idea of the meaning of Christianity. Fanatic in his zeal, he led the break from this tradition to the beautiful simplicity of the Cistercian order.

Vézelay and Fontenay

Sue's and my two favorite sites are Vézelay and Fontenay, supreme examples of the different style of the two orders. The monastery of the former, the Basilica of St. Mary Magdalene, was founded in the ninth century and came under control of the Benedictine Abbey, Cluny, in the eleventh century. It sits atop a hill west of the Yonne River, very convenient for bargers on that waterway. From this site, St. Bernard launched the Second Crusade in 1146 in the presence of King Louis VII of France and a gathering of powerful barons. His summons was so compelling that all who heard it embarked at once on this mission. Later, in 1190, Richard the Lion-Hearted and King Philip of France met here to start out on the Third Crusade. As the shelter for the relics of Mary Magdalene to which many miraculous cures were attributed, Vézelay was one of the great places of pilgrimage and a starting point for pilgrims going as far as Santiago de Compostela in Spain. It was also chosen by St. Francis of Assisi for the location of the first of his monasteries. The attraction of Vézelay to pilgrims diminished with the discovery at the end of the thirteenth century of other relics of Mary Magdalene at St.-Maximin in Provence.

Sue and I had visited Vézelay twice on previous travels before this barge trip. We would happily have returned for a third visit, when we were close by in Clamecy, but we agreed with skipper Tom that our tight time schedule to reach our final destination in Chitry would not allow this diversion.

Sublimely contrasting with Vézelay, the lovely Cistercian Abbey of Fontenay is now restored and looks much as it might have in 1118 when it was built. Known as "the Second Daughter of St. Bernard," it was one of three major religious settlements he founded. Having survived the religious wars and the French Revolution when it was sold and transformed into a paper mill, it now exudes the sense of tranquillity and peace that its founders must have intended. The 1906 restoration did away with the paper mill additions, followed the twelfth-century plans in the layout of the complex, and rebuilt the lovely fountains that gave the abbey its name. The church, though not grand in dimensions, inspires all who enter with its monastic simplicity, an austere and timeless grandeur. Other parts of the complex on view include the cloisters, the

dormitory where the monks slept on straw pallets, the chapter house, and the kitchen.

The Benedictine Monasteries

Since the Benedictines operated without the constraints imposed by St. Bernard for the Cistercians, it is not surprising that they attracted to their order far greater numbers of adherents. The world-famous liqueur bearing the Benedictines' name could have originated only with that order, never with the Cistercians, who among their numerous pledges of self-denial took the vow of abstention from all spirits. Their regulations also prohibited eating meat, fish, eggs, milk dishes, and white bread!

Benedictine rules were far more relaxed both in matters of daily regimen and on such questions as architectural standards. Their monasteries, most of which preceded those of the Cistercians, tended to be grander and more lavishly decorated. For example, Cluny, regarded as the high point of medieval spirituality and the pride of the Benedictines, was the largest church in Christendom before St. Peter's was built in

Rome, with five naves and five bell towers and vaults standing more than 100 feet high. Ten thousand monks were under its authority, living not only in the Cluny monastery but also in over a thousand dependencies scattered through the countryside. Its powerful abbots, reporting only to the Holy See, were independent of temporal authority. For the same reasons that St. Bernard left the Benedictines, the order began to decline when the lack of discipline in their way of life came under harsh criticism in the secular world. The best evidence of their lavish lifestyle can be found today in the mansion now known as the Cluny Museum acquired for their representatives in Paris. The grand scale and elaborate decoration of this edifice attest to the luxurious lifestyle of the powerful clerics sent by the Benedictines as their ambassadors to Paris.

Although Cluny abbey, located in the southeastern corner of Burgundy just off the N79 to the northwest of Mâcon, was virtually destroyed in the Revolution, substantial ruins still convey a vivid sense of its enormous scale and magnificence. The Abbot's palace, built during the same period as the Cluny mansion in Paris, now houses a museum displaying items excavated over the centuries and models of the huge complex as it appeared before the Revolution.

West of Cluny abbey is another smaller Benedictine monastery, Paray-le-Monial. Since it was extensively restored during the nineteenth and twentieth centuries, it gives today's visitor a vivid sense of the architecture and lifestyle of the Benedictines.

La Charité-sur-Loire, in the Nivernais on the western border of Burgundy on the N7, is the second oldest Benedictine monastery, and also the biggest after Cluny. Its name derives from the generosity of its monks to the area poor. Much of La Charité still remains standing, and it is another example of Benedictine style surviving over the centuries and well worth a visit. From Clamecy, it is only about an hour's drive on the N151 to La Charité.

Guédelon, a Medieval Castle Only Now Being Built

Another way of capturing a sense of the Middle Ages in Burgundy is to visit the castle of Guédelon near Saint Fargeau in the Yonne, southwest of Auxerre on the D90. This imaginative creation is the brainchild of an enterprising landowner, Michel Guyot, who conceived the idea of building an authentic version of an early thirteenth-century castle using only materials and techniques available at that period. With a plan drawn by the Historical Monuments Administration and the financial support of a few sponsors, this castle/fortress is now slowly taking shape in a wooded site not far from an abandoned quarry. A team of highly skilled artisans—stonecutters, carpenters, smiths, and masons—guided by a committee of historians and archeologists is painstakingly recreating a castle that might have been built in the reign of King Philippe Auguste. Adamantly disdaining any techniques or tools invented after the period of the project, they have reconstructed everything from levers and saws to ropes and water containers using only know-how that would have been available eight centuries ago. By the same token, project leaders have rejected such a contemporary concept as a deadline for completion, so no one knows quite when it will be finished or exactly how it will look. What is already apparent, however, is that the project has struck a responsive chord with the public which have been coming in droves to see this evocation of a fascinating era of Burgundy's past.

The Duchy of Burgundy at Its Peak of Power

Burgundy's peak of power and prestige occurred somewhat later than that of the Guédelon recreation. It lasted a little over 100 years (1364–1477) under the Valois dynasty, the Grand Dukes of the West as they were called, Philip the Bold *(Philippe le Hardi)*, John the Fearless *(Jean Sans Peur)*, Philip the Good *(Philippe le Bon)*, and Charles the Bold *(Charles le Téméraire)*. These rulers skillfully applied a strategy designed to expand their dominion over an ever-increasing territory until it became the single greatest geopolitical center in all of Europe. The strategy included some bloody military conquests, alliances with other powerful ruling houses on Burgundy's borders, and calculated intermarriages with some of those houses.

Philip the Bold (1364–1404)

Philip the Bold, for example, married the richest heiress in Europe, Margaret of Flanders, thereby acquiring not only a huge fortune but also the territory of Flanders on the North Sea, which encompassed much of present-day Holland and Belgium plus Artois. Margaret was far from being a great beauty, but Philip was willing to overlook her plainness for the sake of her fortune. He also willingly led Burgundy soldiers in skirmishes to put down uprisings of Flemish citizens in order to please Margaret's father who, on his death, generously remembered his son-in-law. Flanders was but one building block in a series of land acquisitions well to the north of Burgundy itself. With his new wealth Philip began the construction of the great ducal palace in Dijon where he lived in sumptuous splendor and attracted to his court painters and sculptors from Flanders and other parts of his dominion. Under his auspices a *Cour Amoureuse* was formed to commemorate Saint Valentine's Day, a kind of honorary society honoring women and fostering poetry, music, and the arts throughout the dukedom.

Philip's brother was King Charles V of France, so, when Charles died, Philip became the leader of the Regency council that ruled France for the young King Charles VI. Duke Philip continued as the virtual ruler of France until his death in 1404.

John the Fearless (1404–19)

Philip's successor as the new Duke of Burgundy was John the Fearless. Before inheriting the Burgundy dukedom, John, then Duke of Nevers, led a disastrous crusade to Jerusalem against the Saracens who soundly defeated his army. John was captured and held prisoner until ransom was paid and he returned to Burgundy. John aspired to the position his father had held as the Regent of France. But his cousin, the rakish womanizer Louis, Duke of Orléans, also claimed that lofty position, so John had him ambushed and bludgeoned to death in a dark alley. This action started the bloody civil war between Burgundians and Armagnacs who supported the Orléans line. John recruited strong-arm ruffians including butchers from Les Halles, the old Paris market, to attack the Armagnacs in a coup that gave him control of Paris. But he did not last long in this powerful position. In 1419, trapped into attending a "peace parley," he was attacked by a hatchet-wielding knight under orders from the Dauphin (later Charles VII), who sought to avenge the murder of the Duke of Orléans and the losses suffered by the Armagnacs.

Philip the Good (1419–67)

Thus the Dukes of Burgundy, with their blood ties to the French throne and their rivalry with unfriendly French cousins, always had to keep a watchful eye on France, which considered Burgundy a logical target for its own expansion. The Burgundy dukes pursued a Machiavellian strategy, sometimes aligning themselves with their arch-rival France while on other occasions siding with France's great nemesis, England. So it came about that John's son, Philip the Good, seeking to avenge his father's murder, made an alliance with the British. One byproduct of this connection involved Joan of Arc. The Burgundians had captured her in the battle of Compiègne. Since the French King Charles VII was too parsimonious to pay her ransom, Philip, playing the English card, agreed to sell her to the British for the enormous sum of 10,000 livres.

Philip the Good had a consuming passion for magnificence in everything that touched his life: his wardrobe, his palatial residences, and the adornments of those palaces. With the proceeds from the sale of the Maid of Orleans, he was able to indulge this passion. He maintained palaces in six cities of his vast dominion. While he referred to Dijon in official documents as his "capital," he actually ruled mainly from Brussels, which was more the epicenter of his dominion. He married three rich women, the third being Isabel of Portugal, and consolidated his rule over not only the Flemish, Dutch, and Belgian territory on France's northern borders but also a strategic belt consisting of Luxembourg, Lorraine, and Alsace between France on the west and the Holy Roman Empire to the east. Partly in acknowledging this strong position, the French Dauphin made peace with Philip, thereby recognizing the virtual independence of Burgundy during the last years of Philip's reign.

Charles the Bold (1467–77)

On Philip's death, the last of the four great dukes of Burgundy, Charles the Bold, sometimes called Charles the Rash, came to power. He inherited Philip's taste for magnificence but also fancied himself a bold warrior in the tradition of Alexander the Great. His military adventures in Alsace and Lorraine to extend his power into what is now Germany were designed to preempt French designs on that area. This brought him the animosity of King Louis XI of France and other powers in that region. Charles's overreaching eventually led to his defeat and death on the battlefield in 1477 and the annexation of Burgundy by France. With the ending of Burgundy's glorious years of sovereignty the region became nominally but somewhat loosely a part of France in an affiliation allowing Burgundy to exercise a considerable degree of autonomy.

Beaune and the Beaune–Dijon Rivalry

One town that did not submit to French sovereignty was Beaune, which before Dijon had been the principal residence of the Dukes of Burgundy. Located some thirty kilometers south of Dijon, Beaune had been an important Roman outpost and later a rival of the much larger Dijon for the position of capital city. An intense animosity grew up between the citizens of the two towns. When Dijon ceded the sovereignty of Burgundy to Paris, Beaune held out until a five-week siege of the city by French forces forced a surrender. Although the rivalry between the two cities continued well into the eighteenth century, the animosity has diminished as each city has gained recognition for its own importance. What remains is mainly a competition for tourism. While Dijon is the larger commercial and administrative center, Beaune boasts two major assets which assure its place on the Burgundian stage. These are the medieval Hôtel-Dieu, the magnificent hospital/hospice founded in 1443, and the thriving wine trade centered on the vineyards of the Côte de Beaune, an illustrious segment of the Côte d'Or.

The Hôtel-Dieu, a famous tourist attraction, is an extraordinary example of high Burgundian–Flemish art perfectly preserved over five centuries and one of the major tourist attractions in all of Burgundy. The Chancellor of the Duchy of Burgundy, Nicolas Rolin, established the charity for the poor and elderly and endowed it with some of the area's most profitable vineyards. It continued to serve as a general hospital until 1971 when it became a combination museum and geriatric facility. The latter was later transferred to a modern facility on the edge of town. Today the throngs of visitors stand in awe as they gaze from the central courtyard at the elaborately decorated high-pitched roofs, dormer windows, and pinnacles of this unique edifice. The richness and intricacy of decoration are carried out in the interior as well. A visitor today is struck by how the founders of the hospital provided a place of grace and beauty for those in their care, whether rich or poor.

The Hôtel-Dieu also plays a central role in Beaune's wine trade. Bequests by local landowners over five centuries have increased the original endowment to a total of 140 acres of *Grand Cru* and *Premier*

Cru vineyards. In its capacity as the wealthy owner of some of France's finest vineyards, the Hôtel-Dieu sponsors the annual wine auction, drawing wine merchants and wine lovers from all over the world. The auction is held on the third Sunday in November, and the coveted tickets are limited to the trade. Those without an invitation can attend only as guests of regular ticket-holders. The proceeds of the auction go to maintenance of the surgical and medical facilities of the new hospital/hospice.

Les Trois Glorieuses

The Beaune wine auction is one of three events steeped in tradition known as *les Trois Glorieuses*. On the Saturday night before the sale, a banquet is held at Clos Vougeot, headquarters of the famed *Chevaliers du Tastevin,* described in chapter 3. The bidding at the auction on the second night is conducted using tapers which are kept alight until the final bid on each lot. The frantic bidding tends to drive prices way up because of the prestige for the vintner associated with offering such a wine on his list. On the third day the bidders adjourn to Meursault for a luncheon banquet of 300 growers, each taking two bottles of their finest vintages. This event is open for reservations by wine lovers willing to pay just under $100 per person. Crowds of oenophiles not attending these exclusive events turn Beaune into a gigantic wine and cheese party, placing a high premium on designated drivers.

The old fortifications circling Beaune are mostly intact, and sections of old houses built partly in the ramparts with lovely gardens add to the allure of this city. Two one-star restaurants head the list of good places to dine, and a number of good hotels serve the tourist trade. During our stay there Sue and I were very happy with our accommodations at Hôtel de la Poste located near the town center. This was our base for visiting both Beaune and Dijon.

The Ducal Palace in Dijon

For nearly two centuries after Charles's death the ducal palace in Dijon stood empty, but today it houses an impressive Fine Arts Museum, which Sue and I visited on our 1998 scouting expedition. The museum is larger and in many ways more important than any other in France outside of Paris. It transports a visitor back to the fifteenth century when some of the complex was constructed under Philip the Bold. The biggest attraction for many visitors, and one that made an indelible impression on us, was the enormous kitchen built in 1435. Six huge fireplaces were used for cooking the various courses of the feasts served to the great crowds assembled by the dukes in their court. Sue and I were reminded of two similar kitchens preserved from the same era—that in the Conciergerie in Paris and the kitchens in the Palace of the Popes in Avignon. Each of the three examples follows a similar architectural configuration in which the whole room comes to a point high in the vaulted ceiling in a big ventilating chimney capable of sucking up the steam and smoke from the several fireplaces. At meal times the master chef sat on a high stool in the center of the kitchen, armed with a heavy spoon to taste every dish and to raise as a threat against any dawdlers on the staff. It takes little imagination to picture the army of cooks and other helpers stoking fires and rushing about to prepare gargantuan feasts for the ducal guests.

After having stood empty for so many years, the palace complex was radically transformed in the seventeenth century when Dijon was at the height of its parliamentary power. The *Palais des Etats* was designed to accommodate sessions of the Three Estates that assembled here every three years from 1688 until the Revolution. What one sees today are embellishments of the original palace designed by Mansart, one of the architects of Versailles, to convey a grander and more sophisticated impression of a ducal residence. On our visit we had too little time to tour the entire complex, but we were able to go up from the kitchens to the next level to see the Guard Room, the principal visual attraction of the museum. This room epitomizes the passion for magnificence of its builder, Philip the Good, whose portrait hangs here. Also on display are treasures such as gilded altar pieces and a Flemish tapestry saved from the ducal burial site destroyed during the Revolution. This mausoleum was built by the first of the great dukes, Philip the Bold, who aspired to create an "almost-royal" repository for the remains of the almost-royal great dukes.

Francis the First (1494–1547)

One of the most extraordinary chapters in the history of Burgundy unfolded during the reign of Francis the First. On coming to the French

throne in 1515, Francis inherited a tangle of long-standing power struggles between France and all of its surrounding neighbors. England, across the channel but sovereign over large areas in the French hexagon, was a constant threat, as were belligerent Spain to the south and the ever-troublesome Holy Roman Empire to the north. This strange Teutonic conglomeration of imperial rule was tied to Spain through a joint monarchy because Charles V was not only Holy Roman Emperor but also King of Spain. Yet another neighbor to the east consisted of the various city-states of the Italian peninsula, including the Vatican, seat of those grand masters of power politics, the Popes. Because of its location in the center of all these squabbling powers, France and its monarch were inevitably drawn into all their machinations for strategic alliances and military adventures. The prospect of enlarging his dominion through Italian conquests preoccupied Francis during the early part of his reign.

In the course of his search for information about his military prospects in Italy, Francis became aware of the work of that extraordinary Italian genius, Leonardo da Vinci. Francis, like his predecessor Louis XII, had taken an active interest in the idea of linking the Atlantic and the Mediterranean through a network of waterways including canals passing

through Burgundy. He discovered a kindred soul in Leonardo. Throughout his lifetime Leonardo was fascinated by the engineering challenges in altering the course of natural waterways. A number of his drawings feature such diversions as designs for straightening the Arno in Florence. He saw the diversion of rivers as a means to assure flood control, enhance commercial traffic, provide for irrigation, and produce hydraulic power. Some of Leonardo's plans so intrigued Francis that in 1516 he provided financial support to the Italian artist, who was also, conveniently, interested in the military possibilities of canal diversions.

Francis stood out among the monarchs of his time for his personal bravery in battle and his remarkable abilities as a commander of forces.

He gloried in the adulation of his troops whom he led courageously with no apparent regard for his own safety. In Italy, the main focus of his ambition for territorial expansion, he won a great victory at Melegnano against a supposedly invincible force of Swiss mercenaries. The battle took place in the first year of Francis's reign, when he was only twenty-one years old. A treaty between France and Switzerland following Melegnano led to a lasting alliance, ensuring that the powerful Swiss army would henceforth serve on the side of France.

Francis received most of the credit for the victory of Melegnano, but there is evidence that some of the strategies were conceived by the inventive mind of Leonardo. In any event, soon after that battle, Leonardo accepted Francis's invitation to move to France, where he spent the last three years of his life. He was given a small but elegant house next to the chateau of Amboise where Francis could be in close contact with his honored guest. Leonardo was considered an ornament in Francis's court, but his days were numbered, and he died in 1519, according to some accounts in his patron's arms.

Ten years later Francis was at war with a new and powerful antagonist, Charles V, Emperor of the Holy Roman Empire and King of Spain, who had forged alliances with several of France's enemies. Charles was the great-grandson of Charles the Bold, last of the great dukes of Burgundy, and he used this rather remote connection to advance his claim to this region. Such a westward extension of his empire would have made it an even more menacing threat to France. In addition to Burgundy, another point of contention between these two monarchs was the Duchy of Milan, which each coveted.

Infatuated with his role as King of Spain, Charles had moved his base from Aachen in Germany to Madrid, where he assumed a lifestyle more Spanish than the Spaniards. He also took control of the powerful Spanish army, preparing it to fight the French for the prize of Milan. The fateful battle of Pavia that ensued took its name from a fortified town, the second city in the Duchy of Milan, that guarded the approach to Milan itself. This battle brought Charles close to his ambition of bringing Burgundy into the Holy Roman Empire.

In the opening skirmish, Francis led a spirited attack on the enemy's advance guard, killing its leader with his lance; and it seemed for quite a while that victory was virtually assured for the French. But Charles's army fought doggedly in a series of isolated battles, and one of the top French commanders, fearing the day was lost, made the fatal mistake of withdrawing his entire force of 10,000 from the field. Even so, Francis with the support of his household cavalry and his most loyal knights, "the bravest of the brave," attacked in the face of arquebuses at point-blank range. When Francis's horse was shot out from under him and he was at the mercy of Spanish troops trying to pierce his armor with their spears, he was offered the chance to surrender to a peer, one of the top commanders of the Imperial army, Viceroy Lannoy of Provence. In accordance with the chivalric code of honor, Francis gained the protection of his captors but lost everything he had been fighting for to his nemesis, Charles. The battle of Pavia was the absolute nadir of Francis's career, bringing Burgundy perilously close to becoming an appendage of the Holy Roman Empire.

Francis, as the embodiment of the chivalric code of honor, counted on his captors to reciprocate in treating him fairly. But this trust was woefully misplaced. While as a captive sovereign Francis did enjoy certain privileges in the amenities in the several prisons where he was held (eventually he wound up in Madrid), Emperor Charles used his power over his prisoner to demand the harshest of terms in return for his release: Burgundy would have to be handed over to Charles; Francis would have to renounce all claims to any part of Italy; a huge ransom would have to be paid; and, perhaps the cruelest cut of all, Francis's two eldest sons would have to be turned over as hostages until all other terms had been satisfied.

Francis thus found to his dismay that Charles would not abide by the chivalric code to deal fairly with a peer. By that code Charles should have accepted payment of ransom and other less onerous penalties as terms for Francis to secure his freedom. Even though Francis acknowledged that he was ultimately responsible for the defeat at Pavia, he could not accept the harsh terms proposed by Charles. The prospect of surrendering Burgundy was anathema to him. In desperation Francis conceived a ploy for agreeing to Charles's terms but, in effect, with his fingers crossed, so that he could renege when the time arrived for implementation. He gained the consent of a small circle of his closest advisors before entering into a solemn agreement to accept all the terms imposed by Charles. The occasion of the signing was marked by a High

Mass celebrated by an Archbishop in Francis's prison cell. Charles was represented by Viceroy Lannoy, to whom Francis had surrendered at Pavia. Francis's two eldest sons were turned over to be held as hostage/prisoners, thereby reinforcing the impression that he would accede to the other provisions.

While the negotiations for Francis's future were under way, the headstrong Emperor Charles became embroiled in a foolish foray into southern Italy. A horrible ransacking of Rome by Imperial forces forced the Pope to cower in the stronghold of Sant Angelo while princes of the church were being slaughtered and troops extorted huge sums from wealthy citizens to spare their lives. Although Charles had won a military victory, the sacking of Rome signaled to his allies that the Emperor had become a menace to established order, and they began to back out of their alliances with him.

Meanwhile, Francis, released from prison, returned to France in triumph as head of a huge retinue of courtiers in exchange for the surrender of his two sons to become hostages. Once back in France and secure on his throne, he took his case to the French parliament, asking its members to advise him whether he should voluntarily return to prison in Spain or repudiate the treaty that he had signed under duress. Not surprisingly, the parliament concluded that he was under no obligation to abide by the treaty and that, in any event, Burgundy was not his to cede away. When word reached Emperor Charles that his prized prisoner had reneged on his pact with the blessing of the French parliament, he erupted in furious outrage. But his ability to effect any change in the French position, given his weakened military posture after his Italian fiasco, was nonexistent. Thus he had no recourse but to accept the terms of a settlement. Under this so-called Ladies Peace, negotiated by Francis's mother, Louise of Savoy, and Charles's Aunt Margaret of Austria, the treaty brought a settlement to all the contentious issues between the two great powers. Charles gave up his claim to Burgundy; Francis yielded his claims to Italian and Flemish territories; and Francis's sons were released from prison on payment of a two million crown ransom. The peaceful resolution of the long feud between two great powers met with almost universal acclaim.

Another clause of the treaty reconfirmed agreement to the marriage of Francis to Eleanor of Spain. Francis went to Bordeaux to greet his bride and to welcome his ransomed sons. The outbreak of peace, the onset of royal nuptials, and the restoration of the glorious reign of Francis occasioned a six-month period of celebration. Nowhere was there more jubilant rejoicing than in Burgundy, which had been saved from annexation to the dreaded nemesis, the Holy Roman Empire.

However, the bitter rivalry between Francis and Charles was not over, and more hostility lay ahead. When Charles paid a state visit to France, he was treated magnanimously by Francis and allowed to pass through on his way to quell a revolt in the city of Ghent. But during the course of his passage through France, Charles became extremely jealous of his host. His eyes were opened to the great popularity Francis enjoyed, the prosperity of the country, and the splendor of successive royal chateaux where he entertained Charles in great style. Francis resisted pleas by some of his advisors to seize Charles as a prisoner or demand conditions for his royal guest's liberty. But once out of France, Charles turned on Francis with yet another threat of war, this time restating his claim to Burgundy. The ensuing battle took place near a small town in the Italian Alps, Ceresole, where the French won a stunning victory, dealing Charles a humiliating defeat.

Burgundy's Central Role in Building the French Canal Network

Back on his throne and inspired by some of the engineering concepts of his friend Leonardo, Francis was able to turn his thoughts to peaceful pursuits and the possibility of linking inland waterways, including canals passing through Burgundy. But it was not until 1606, nearly sixty years after Francis's death, that the first steps were taken with the construction of a canal linking Dijon to the town of St. Jean-de-Losne several kilometers to the southwest. The first boat coming through from the Saône to the port of Dijon arrived in 1608.

The canal was finally extended more than two hundred years later, linking the Saône and the Yonne. The engineering challenges presented by this project were formidable because of a large and seemingly impenetrable granite formation at Pouilly-en-Auxois, the highest point on the canal's course. It confounded all the experts, as one plan after another to circumvent the mass of solid rock proved infeasible. Finally it was deemed necessary to bore a big hole through the cliffs. A straight line tunnel 3.333 kilometers long was cut through the rocks by manual laborers using the crude tools of the era. Many lost their lives or were critically injured in the process. To ventilate the canal required the sinking of thirty-two air holes from the surface, which at some points was fifty yards above the canal. The project took a total of six years to complete. The full length of the Burgundy canal was finished in 1837 under King Louis-Philippe, the last of the French kings, thus providing a link of vital logistical importance between Lyon and Paris. Support for the enterprise was provided by every ruler of France beginning with Henri IV.

Erasing the Name of Burgundy

After the French Revolution, the name of Burgundy was formally abolished because it represented so many years of rivalry with France. However the Burgundians themselves continued to use the name, mainly because their wine retained its name, which was what really mattered to them. The name did not regain official use until 1964 when General de Gaulle grouped the ninety departments of France into twenty-eight regions for economic planning. The four departments of Burgundy are Yonne, Côte d'Or, Saône-et-Loire, and Nièvre.

In the latter part of the nineteenth century, all French canals were made to conform to what is known as the Freycinet standard governing the dimensions of locks, water depths, draught of vessels, etc. Charles Louis de Freycinet, minister of public works from 1877 to 1879, took the initiative to classify French waterways as either principal or secondary routes, establishing standards for the construction and maintenance of the system. Meeting these standards required a massive program of widening and deepening channels, rebuilding locks, and raising bridges. Thanks to Freycinet, the proportions of French waterways are generous in comparison to those of the UK, for example.

Just as canals were becoming vital links for commercial traffic, railroads were being built, and competition between the two modes of transport developed. Nevertheless, for several decades after its completion, the Burgundy canal remained an important commercial waterway, although today such traffic has almost completely disappeared. Now, as it passes through a succession of beautiful Burgundian landscapes, the canal has become a favorite of pleasure craft. Those fortunate enough to travel on the waterways of Burgundy should be aware of the deep roots of history in the land they are traversing, how every town through which they pass played a part in that history, and how each new vista of their route can reveal not only the glories of natural landscapes but also man-made structures ranging from simple farm buildings to grand chateaux and impressive ecclesiastical sites.

TWO 🍇
From St-Florentin to Chitry in a Week

What IS a Barge?

To the uninitiated, the word "barge" may connote cumbersome commercial vessels sometimes seen, often rusting along the banks, on American waterways. The barges used as pleasure boats on European canals are domesticated versions of these vessels quite like houseboats. In fact, the French word *péniche* means both barge and houseboat. Quite a few pleasure barges on European waterways have been converted from old commercial vessels as were the two hotel barges on which Sue and I had cruised, while newer ones are built specifically to serve the growing market for barging. The charter companies also offer models of cabin cruisers with a more contemporary look and pointed bows which can be more responsive to the helm. They may also go faster than barges, though speed limits on the canals apply to all vessels. It is very bad form to create sizable waves in your wake.

In choosing your vessel, whether barge or cabin cruiser, it's useful to consider where the helm is located. We had no problems on our barge with the helm in the bow on the lower deck. Other boaters may prefer being able to steer from the top deck where you can get a better view of the oncoming locks.

Stocking up the Barge

Through The Barge Broker in Colorado we signed up with the French barge operator, Rive de France, to charter a barge for a week in mid-June starting in St-Florentin and ending in Chitry. The Colorado firm sent us a considerable amount of literature, including a thirty-one-page *Captain's Manual,* with instructions on preparation for departure, boat handling, safety, waterman's glossary, and directions to our marina. Another twenty-seven-page illustrated brochure, *Relaxing on the*

Waterways, contained charts and other data on the several routes on which Rive de France operated its barges. A hefty 216-page *Guide Vagnon de Tourisme Fluvial* published by the French yachting association provided details on each segment of the route we would follow, including distances between ports and locks, width of waterways, type of locks, and amenities such as marina facilities and restaurants of the towns where we would be stopping. We also received a half dozen reprints of articles on the history, geography, and attractions of the terrain we would be passing through. An important consideration in selecting a charter company is the amount and quality of information they provide for prospective bargers.

We had selected this particular route for several reasons: a) it was available in the limited time frame when all family members could be on board, b) a barge that could accommodate all seven of us could be chartered then, and c) we wanted to cruise one-way rather than round-trip. Our barge class was *Eau Claire 1400,* and our barge was named the *Matisse,* a name that resonated with the artist in me. It had taken the better part of six months to find the best charter company, select a time when all seven of our family members were free to travel, and line up the charter.

The charter company provided a list of all the items they furnish for each boat, including safety items such as life jackets, boat hooks, and fire extinguisher as well as "comfort items," meaning galley and dining implements, cleaning materials, bedding, etc. All food and drink, including the staples, must be provided by the bargers. Since galley storage space is limited, we could not stock up big items for more than one or two days at a time. Sue and Nancy, both serious cooks, good organizers, and experienced sailors, developed an appropriate shopping list for our cruise, taking into account everyone's food preferences. Since the girls consume untold gallons of bottled water, it almost required a special detail to haul the bottles on board each day and then dispose of the empties.

The Cast of Characters

It's impossible to imagine a better group of traveling companions than the five who came with us. While admitting a certain subjective bias in their favor, the objective fact is that they all measured up in every way

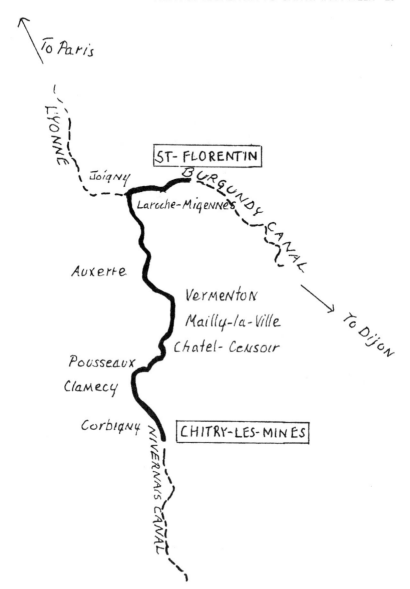

To Paris

L'YONNE

ST-FLORENTIN

Joigny

BURGUNDY CANAL

Laroche-Migennes

Auxerre

VERMENTON

Mailly-la-Ville

Chatel-Censoir

To Dijon

Pousseaux

Clamecy

Corbigny

CHITRY-LES-MINES

NIVERNAIS CANAL

to the codes one hopes for on the part of shipmates living in close quarters. Son-in-law Tom, a globe-trotting businessman, has just the temperament needed by a barge captain: imperturbable in all situations, cool-headed and relaxed, and possessed of a delightfully wry sense of humor. He brought out the best in all of us who served under his command as crew.

Nancy was an ideal mate, having sailed as much as she had with Tom in Maine and having learned how to run a "tight ship" at home in Connecticut. A disciplinarian with a light touch, she, with Tom's strong backing, has raised three daughters with impeccable manners— what every parent or grandparent would hope for. Nancy is a close copy of my wife, as the French say, *Comme mère, comme fille,* organized to a tee, an enthusiastic shopper, a gourmet cook, and a committed civic activist.

The three siblings have remarkably distinctive personalities and interests. All are bright, good-looking, and fun to be with, but each in her own way. At the time of our cruise, Kate of the smashing red locks was about to enter her senior year of high school as a popular leader of her class, with a legion of male admirers. Her biggest outside interest is modern dance.

Second daughter Perrin is the gifted creative sister. Painting and writing are favorite outlets for her talent. Fascinated by dolphins and other creatures of the deep, Perrin had come with Sue and me on a couple of trips to Key West to swim with the dolphins.

Julia is the athlete of the trio, a star in every sport she has taken up. But ice hockey is her passion, and she is so good in that tough competition that she qualifies to play on boys' teams.

All three girls were agile line handlers and nimble climbers on the lock ladders. As noted earlier, Julia became the one responsible for tipping the lockkeepers. While this crew was exceptionally well equipped to handle the barge, it is worth repeating that prior boating experience is *not* a prerequisite for barging.

The Day Before Departure

Sue and I picked up a rental car at Orly Airport below Paris, which we had chosen because it is much closer than De Gaulle Airport to St-Florentin, our port of departure. For the night before the barge pickup, we had reserved a room in St-Florentin's charming one-star hotel, Grande Chaumière. This small (only ten guest rooms) hotel has a cozy understated ambiance, and we were equally pleased by its restaurant where we dined that night. Chef Bonvalot has sent us one of his favorite recipes which Sue has adapted as follows:

 Scallops Grande Chaumière
Serves 4

16 large sea scallops
2 tablespoons clarified butter
¼ cup fish fumet* or bottled clam juice
3 tablespoons strong Italian-style expresso coffee
3 tablespoons crème fleurette (crème fraiche or sour cream)
2 tablespoons cold unsalted butter

Rinse scallops and pat dry. Lightly dust with flour. Heat clarified butter and saute scallops over medium to high heat until lightly browned on each side. This must be done very quickly.

Boil fish fumet or clam juice 3 minutes or so to reduce a little. Add expresso coffeee; boil 1 minute. Whisk in crème fleurette, and boil 3 or 4 minutes to allow mixture to thicken slightly. Off heat, stir in cold butter. Spoon some sauce on four plates or a platter, place scallops on top, and finish by drizzling rest of sauce over all.

Chef Bonvalot recommends one or more of the following vegetables, all julienned and steamed, to accompany this dish: white cabbage, red cabbage, celery root.

*This is a stock made with fish trimmings and other flavorings. In a restaurant kitchen it is usually available, but the home cook may wish to substitute bottled clam juice.

The next morning was devoted to shopping at the *Intermarché* in St-Florentin. Just as we returned to the hotel with the groceries, the van carrying our crewmates from De Gaulle airport pulled up to the hotel entrance. After warm greetings we showed the new arrivals to our hotel room where they could make themselves at home while we went off to turn in our rental car in Auxerre. The Hertz office there was closed for the two-hour lunch break which we took as an excuse to head for a restaurant. The prospect did not upset us in the slightest since we had previously discovered the attractive Barnabet, where we returned happily on this occasion.

Barnabet

In Auxerre, the capital of Yonne, and a major stopping place for bargers, one might expect to find quite a number of good restaurants, but Barnabet is the single one-star establishment. Sue and I have especially enjoyed dining on the outdoor terrace. The restaurant is right off the waterfront but enough removed from the traffic to provide a secluded atmosphere. Along the corridor leading to the dining area, a glass wall reveals a splendid modern kitchen.

Although we were not staggered by the prices, *La Belle France* in its May 1995 issue warned that they were excessive except for the wine list with its impressive selection of Burgundies. However, that article praises two special dishes: langoustines (the little crustaceans the Italians call scampi) served with strips of ginger soaked in *ratafia* (a light locally made liqueur blending grape juice and *marc de Bourgogne*), and a rack of lamb with garlic mashed potatoes which is among the dishes recommended in the red Michelin guide.

Chef Barnabet sent us one of his house recipes.

 Adapted from Jean-Luc Barnabet's Recipe for
Fruits in Chablis Jelly
Serves 8

Fruits:
1½ cups fresh strawberries
6 oranges
3 grapefruits

Mousse:
½ cup fresh lemon juice
grated rind of 2 lemons
2 eggs
scant ½ cup sugar
1½ tablespoons butter, melted

Chablis jelly:
2 teaspoons gelatin
2 oz. sugar
zest of ½ orange thinly peeled
1½ cups Chablis

1. To prepare the mousse:

In a bowl set over simmering water, place all mousse ingredients except the butter. Whisk vigorously until foamy (about 3 minutes). Add melted butter, whisking. Distribute mousse on bottoms of 8 dessert bowls.

2. To prepare fruits and jellied Chablis:

Place sugar and orange zest in food processor and process until zest is almost pulverized. Place in large saucepan with the Chablis and heat slowly. Sprinkle with the gelatin, and when gelatin is melted, heat and stir until sugar is dissolved. Do not boil. Remove from heat. Cool and refrigerate until liquid has begun to jell. Peel and section citrus fruits and let drain in a colander.

3. To assemble the dessert:

Place strawberries and citrus sections on top of the mousse and around sides of dessert bowls. Pour some of the not-quite-jelled Chablis over the fruit and refrigerate for one hour. Then cover with remaining Chablis and refrigerate until ready to serve—at least one hour.

After lunch we taxied back to the Rive de France marina in St-Florentin where the rest of our crew had been loading our supplies on the *Matisse* and checking out the cabin accommodations, galley layout, two toilets, shower units, and other essentials. Since the capacity of barge water tanks is limited, we were warned to fill the tank at every opportunity. On the other hand, there was enough fuel at the start to last until the end of our charter, when we were expected to fill up for the next bargers. Since Skipper Tom had been given the rundown on operation of the boat, we were ready to take off on the first leg of our trip under a bright blue sky.

Accommodations

This diagram from the Rive de France brochure depicts the layout of our forty-one-foot barge. The aft cabin, though small, was the most spacious, and the rest of the crew had already decided while we were in Auxerre that it should be assigned to Sue and me as the hosts of the cruise. It had a small wash basin, as did two other cabins, a convenience that relieved pressure on the heads. Although the *Eau Claire 1400* class is advertised as large enough to sleep a maximum of nine, somehow we seemed to use all the sleeping spaces with just seven normal size bodies. One lesson we learned from our experience is that claims of maximum capacity in barge company literature should not be confused with maximum comfort levels. We managed happily enough, but it took a willing and patient crew to work things out. The two younger girls shared one cabin. Nancy and Tom had another cabin, but since it was pretty cramped, Tom opted to sleep in the forward cabin on cushions that made into a bed. Kate drew a bunk no bigger than a large box, so she chose to sleep on cushions along the fore-to-aft passageway opposite the galley. Her arrangement worked well during the night, but when morning came and people started moving forward for break-

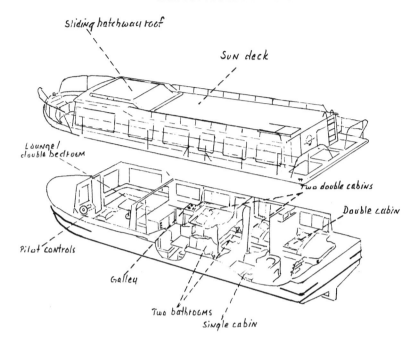

Sliding hatchway roof

Sun deck

Lounge/double bedroom

Two double cabins

Double cabin

Pilot controls

Galley

Two bathrooms

Single cabin

fast, Kate would carry her pillow into the cabin vacated by Nancy not to emerge for another hour or so.

Tom was always up early, rearranging his bed cushions to fit around the lounge table and doing the other chores boat captains find imperative. On days when we had a long way to go, he would start off before the rest of us had finished breakfast. Sue might spell him at the helm so that he could catch a bite to eat, and sometimes he turned the helm over to other crew members. Considering all the time he had to spend on charting each day's course and time spent at the helm, each break was richly deserved.

Negotiating Locks

Charter companies provide charts of the waterways with precise information on the location and type of locks along the route you have selected. Lock opening hours vary with the time of year and between waterways. Generally speaking, lockkeepers are on duty from 6 AM to 7:30 PM with a one-hour break for the midday meal, though the hour may sometimes stretch out. Barges approach the lock on a first-come, first-served basis, lining up to await the lockkeeper's go-ahead to enter. The procedure for passing through locks depends on whether you are locking downstream or upstream. Charter companies provide instructions in their manuals for each process. A helpful interactive animation on locking is presented on the Burgundy Canal site listed in Appendix C. The following excerpt is taken from the *Rive de France Captain's Handbook*.

Locking Downstream

1. The boat enters the lock. The lockkeeper closes the gates upstream.
2. The lockkeeper opens the sluices downstream to lower the water level. The crew member on shore keeps an eye on the ropes that will be kept loose as the boat goes down.
3. The downstream gates are open. The crew member on shore uses the ladder to get back on board.

Make sure the lock is ready (that is when the lock gates are open) and enter the lock slowly; never try to enter adrift. Remember if your propeller does not turn, you are unable to handle your boat. Once the boat is in the middle of the lock, give a short burst of reverse gear to stop the boat and loop your bow rope, then your stern rope to the bollards, slackening them to allow the boat to drop two or four meters with the water level. The upstream gates shut, the lockkeeper gradually opens the downstream sluices, so that the water level drops. Then the gates reopen and you may cast off. Take care to keep your ropes orderly on the deck (with no ropes trailing in the water).

Anyone left on shore can rejoin the boat by means of the lock ladder (which can be slippery) or by means of the stairway outside the lock gates. Never jump on the roof: it can be dangerous for you and cause damage to the boat. It is also possible to pick up the crew member(s) about a hundred meters beyond the lock: this is by far the less perilous way since it avoids the use of a slippery ladder or stairway.

Locking Upstream

The process is the same as downstream but in reverse order, since the boat enters the lock at lower level and leaves it at upper level. It is advisable to set down at least one crew member (about one hundred meters before the lock) who will moor the boat and help the lockkeeper. There is sometimes a four-meter difference in level, and not all the locks have ladders; therefore, it is necessary to put one or two crew members ashore before entering the lock.

1. The boat slowly enters the lock, one or two crew members having been set down 100 meters before the lock.
2. The pilot, having stopped the boat, throws the ropes to the crew members on shore who loop them around the bollards, throwing the ends back to people on board.
3. One person on shore shuts the downstream gate; the pilot holds on to the mooring ropes strongly to keep the boat motionless as water is pouring through the sluices.
4. The lockkeeper opens the sluices; as the boat goes up, the pilot tightens the mooring ropes, especially the bow line, to prevent the boat from moving backwards and hitting the gate.
5. When the lock is full, the crew member(s) on shore opens the upstream gate at a signal given by the lockkeeper, and the pilot coils up the ropes and puts them on the deck. The crew members reboard, and the boat leaves the lock slowly.

All these explanations may seem difficult, but don't be afraid: handling a boat is a matter of common sense and logic only.

Day 1, St-Florentin to Brienon (Shakedown Cruise)

On the basis of his prior study of the chart in the *Captain's Manual*, Tom had chosen Brienon as our first port of call. It would be an easy shakedown cruise, being only 9.3 kilometers from St-Florentin with just four locks to negotiate. Moreover, the manual recommended it as a quiet well-equipped harbor, and the marina staff had given us the name of a good restaurant there. In high spirits we cast off, waved goodbye to St-Florentin, and began our adventure. Sue and Nancy were experienced sailors, and all the years of sailing in Maine with their father were instantly evident in the granddaughters' seamanship. They took to handling the barge lines like veterans. They knew the best nautical knots; they did not have to be told to coil the lines at the cleats; and they kept the decks free of debris. Even though such know-how was not a prerequisite, it was a big plus to have these three well-trained crewmates.

Our shakedown cruise went off without a hitch. On debarking at Brienon, I was assigned to find the restaurant recommended by the marina staff in St-Florentin. I took off with visions in my head of the perfect supper to satisfy a hungry crew in a charming restaurant. Soon I saw off to the right of the main street a large gold-lettered sign for what appeared to be an elegant restaurant in an attractive park-like setting. This must be the place, I thought. On entering, however, I noticed lots of elderly people seated around tables jammed together in something like a nursing home setting. When the woman in charge approached me and I explained my mission, she said that she was *desolée,* but the restaurant had been converted to a retirement home. She gave me the name of the only other restaurant in town that would be open.

Disheartened by my failure to find the ideal restaurant for our first night but desperate to find some place to eat, I trudged up the long hill of the main street toward the one open establishment. My heart sank more than a little on finding this sorry excuse for a restaurant, accessible only through a smoke-filled bar where some rather seedy local customers were hanging out. They eyed me with something between curiosity and contempt for a stranger intruding on their terrain. Reluctantly, I reserved a table for our crew, walked down the hill, and reported my bad news to the group on board the *Matisse.* Politely repressing their disappointment, they fell in line behind me and we walked up the hill to dinner.

The kindest thing I can say about our dinner was that it kept us from starving. Most of us ordered *faux-filet* (a sirloin cut) with *frites* (French fries), some tough canned asparagus, and a very ordinary *vin ordinaire.* In comparison with the meal we had been anticipating it was quite a letdown. The experience corroborated what Sue and I had already learned more than once—that it is entirely possible to have a bad meal in France.

Day 2, Brienon-Gurgy (and Swan-Avoidance)

Tom got us off to an early start, then after a while turned the helm over to Sue on a placid stretch of the canal. She sighted a group of

swans up ahead and, as a nature lover, steered a course to port hoping not to disturb them. This course change resulted in swinging the stern on to the bank where long heavy grass was growing in the water. Tom took the wheel while Nancy leapt to the bank and, with superhuman exertion, used the boat hook to shove the stern back into midstream. But soon after getting back under way, Tom noticed that he was losing headway and steerage.

To find out what the problem was, we tied up on the opposite side of the canal, and Tom removed the hatch over the small engine compartment where the propeller box was lodged. Turning himself upside down, he lowered his torso into this tight space, with only his feet and legs up in the air. He used one arm to support himself in this ungainly position while with the other he removed the top of the propeller box and began pulling out wads of the thick grass that had begun to wind around the propeller shaft. After a suspenseful eternity in which a sizable pile of grass had accumulated on deck, Tom struggled his way back to an upright position on deck. However, he had not been able to remove all of the grass, and much worse, he had found that the real culprit was some wire mesh the propeller had hit, now hideously wound in a tangle around its shaft.

Since there were no wire clippers on board, we walked a couple of hundred yards to the nearest lockkeeper's house at Migennes and borrowed a pair. Tom reinserted himself in his upside-down position and tried to cut the offending wire tangle, but the clippers were not up to the job. Time was passing, and we were not making the progress we counted on for our first full day. At that point we resorted to a remedy that we probably should have tried as soon as our trouble began, phoning the Rive de France marina in St-Florentin and requesting a mechanic. In only about fifteen minutes a "wiry" (unavoidable pun) young man drove up. He was a good deal smaller than Tom and could fit into the engine compartment more easily and managed to free the propeller shaft of its tangle quite readily. The lesson we learned from this misadventure is that, even though you may feel isolated in another world on your barge, help is only minutes away. Now, in hindsight, I can see that this would have been just the time to have had a handy cell phone on board.

Under way again, we proceeded through three more locks on the Burgundy canal to LaRoche where we turned south on the Yonne River. Another six locks took us to the town of Gurgy where we tied up for the night along with a throng of other bargers. A little brochure, *Gurgy Pratique*, welcomed us to this pleasant little town of some 1600 inhabitants and advertised the only restaurant, the Hôtel-restaurant de la Rivière.

Close to our mooring was a group of attractive houses with well-tended flower and vegetable gardens. When we paused to admire the flowers with the most brilliant colors, Sue, the serious gardener, cried out "Oops!" There among the flowers she had spotted the unmistakable foliage of cannabis (marijuana), growing in front of a prim and proper house. We wondered whether this plant had lots of company elsewhere but decided against further investigation. Instead, we followed the *Gurgy Pratique* directions to the restaurant, situated on the Place de l'Eglise. More well-tended and colorful gardens lined the pedestrian path to the Place, which in years gone by was the village cemetery and now serves as a town square with park benches. The thirteenth to sixteenth century church dedicated to Saint André is the oldest and most significant edifice overlooking the square.

The restaurant, a few steps from the church, had an unassuming but welcoming atmosphere, and many fellow bargers were already dining there when we arrived. The menu offered a combination of traditional Burgundy fare with some more contemporary innovations, all of which whetted the appetites of our famished crew. The girls confidently ordered their dinners in French. This time we had found the kind of place we'd dreamed of, we'd succeeded in overcoming our first crisis, and we felt we had finally hit our stride.

Day 3, Gurgy to Auxerre (Town of Art and History)

The highlight of this day was our stop in Auxerre, the capital of the Yonne, the seat of the bishops of Auxerre, and by far the largest town we would visit on our trip. Since Sue and I had been so favorably impressed on our previous visits, we were eager to show the rest of our crew some of the principal sights. However, there were five locks that we had to pass through on leaving Gurgy, and it was late morning before we tied up in the port of Auxerre. As indicated on the map, the main waterway north of Auxerre is the Yonne River, while to the south it is the Nivernais canal alongside of which the Yonne wanders. The port of Auxerre offers a wide range of facilities including a public bath-house, near which we tied up in the hope of using showers there later in the day. We walked across the footbridge leading from the marina to the old town.

Some History

Built on a hillside overlooking the river Yonne, Auxerre's most striking architectural feature is a skyline dominated by two enormous churches,

St. Stephen's Cathedral (also known as Cathédral St-Etienne) and the
Church of St. Germanus (or St. Germain). Each of these buildings rises
over the remains of early structures, St. Stephen's over the fourth-
century sanctuary of St. Amâtre and St. Germanus over a sixth-century
Benedictine Abbey built by Queen Clotilda, wife of Clovis. A steep
climb over winding cobblestoned streets leads from the waterfront up
to the level of the two ancient churches. Old houses, some half-
timbered, look out over these streets as they have for centuries.

Germanus, or St. Germain as he is known in France, is one of the
most popular of French saints. A lawyer from a rich family in Auxerre,
he was practicing law in Rome when he was sent back to his home
town as military adviser. There he underwent a remarkable conversion
to Christianity, so intense that he gave up sharing his bed with his wife,

slept on bare planks, wore a hair shirt, and lived on three meals of coarse bread a week. Although being a Christian in his era was risky, Germanus managed to become a brilliant bureaucrat and a zealous protector of the faith against heretics.

Auxerre's historical roots dip back into antiquity; and, in the era of Roman empire, the Agrippan Way intersecting with the Yonne River made this a busy crossroad. After the Romans, waves of Germanic invasions led Auxerre to withdraw from the riverbank up the hill which was fortified in a succession of walled strongholds. St. Germain initiated the building of monasteries around Auxerre whose walls also served to enclose and protect the town. By the Middle Ages, the secular and religious properties formed a single urban complex. At this time the most important economic activities were viticulture, farming, and floating lumber downstream to Paris. Huge rafts of lumber were formed upstream in Clamecy and at flood water floated down the Yonne through Auxerre where additional rafts were added. The handling of this *flottage* enterprise and the transporting of other goods required a labor force of watermen, and the business of this canal port remains an economic mainstay of Auxerre to this day.

Sightseeing

There was just enough time before lunch for a brief tour of St. Stephen's Cathedral. We paused to view the tympanum over the center door and the lintel depicting the Last Judgment, with the Wise Virgins on Christ's right and the Foolish Virgins holding lamps upside down on the left. Some of the other sculptures on the façade show the damage wrought during the Wars of Religion when the Huguenots took Auxerre in 1567. Two great rose windows on the north and south transepts and the rows of stained glass medallions on the ambulatory bathed the interior with glorious color. Down in the eleventh-century crypt with its early Gothic vaulted ceiling, we saw the cathedral's most famous mural of Christ on horseback. Nearby, the Bishops' Palace and several canonical buildings enhance the space surrounding the cathedral.

Having fed the soul with this uplifting tour, we looked around the cathedral square for a promising place for lunch. Here we were in the center of a lovely French town where presumably there was no dearth of good French restaurants, but somehow all of our eyes fastened on a rather good-looking modern building across the square—an Italian pizza place! At least it was not Pizza Hut, McDonald's, or Burger King, and it did have very good pizzas to satisfy seven healthy appetites. With no shame for our choice of cuisine, we dined with gusto on our delicious pizzas.

Now it was time for some marketing because we had decided to have dinner on board the *Matisse* that evening. We acquired some baguettes and cheeses from small specialty shops, along with *paté*, quiches, and fruit tarts from a *traiteur* (delicatessen), and other necessities such as bottled water and wine from the Monoprix supermarket. Auxerre is in the heart of the Chablis vineyard region, and we tried out a series of different Chablis vintages during the course of our cruise. A wine cellar near the Office of Tourism on the Auxerre waterfront, *Quai de la République,* offers wine tastings.

A principal attraction of Auxerre which we admired after shopping was the fifteenth-century clock tower on the *rue de l'Horloge*. The building of this flamboyant Gothic ornament symbolizes the rise of the bourgeoisie in a town previously dominated by the nobles and clergy. The Count of Auxerre, in giving the clock and its mechanism to the town, also granted communal liberties to its inhabitants.

We wound our way down the hill and back across the footbridge to the *Matisse*. Some took showers in the bathhouse where you didn't need to conserve water and where the space was less cramped than on board. Sue and Nancy began preparations for our one and only dinner afloat—a delicious smorgasbord of all the delicacies we had purchased in Auxerre. That evening brought a heavy rain, but we were snug and secure in our barge, hoping for a bright sun the next day.

Day 4, Auxerre to Châtel-Censoir on the Nivernais Canal

Our hopes were brilliantly fulfilled, and we cast off from Auxerre well before other barges were getting under way. By now certain routines had been established. Tom was always up early preparing for takeoff, and I was in the bow helping him with the bow lines. Sue and Nancy were in the galley preparing breakfast while the three girls, figuring that vacation is a time for sleeping late, rose after we were well under way, but in time to help with the first lock. They nimbly scrambled up the lock ladders to catch the lines tossed up from below and loop them

around the bollards. Julia was soon designated as tip-giver and conducted a daily shakedown of other crew members to collect tip money.
Although bargers are expected to assist the lockkeeper in operating the
lock gates, the custom at the time of our cruise was to offer a tip of
about two or three francs. Now we understand that inflation has driven
up tip expectations to four or five francs, and one ungrateful lockkeeper

is reported to have thrown a two-franc tip back on a barge. Most lockkeepers welcome an exchange of banter and a word of thanks, and we always wish them *bonne journée* on leaving. Today we were aiming to go through ten locks.

Our first stop was in the town of Vincelles where the pictograph on the *Guide Vagnon* showed there would be a grocery store. This one was a very small outlet of the Casino chain which also has larger stores in some of the larger towns. This one had all the essentials we needed, plus a very agreeable local wine *Pouilly Vincelles*. Sue and I took down our bikes and rode along the towpath. Kate and Perrin, determined to keep their trim figures, went for a jog. The Nivernais lived up to its reputation as one of the most scenic and tranquil waterways in France. One of its distinctive appeals stems from the tradition of planting fruit and nut trees along the banks. Proceeds from the crops were used to help defray running expenses in early days, but seven trees on each side of the lock houses were granted to the lockkeepers.

Most of the fruit trees have by now been overtaken by willows, plane trees, linden trees, and oaks which grow in dense forests sometimes arching over the canal. On most days we heard bird songs as we drifted silently along. Between the stands of trees, we passed numerous meadows and open spaces with cattle grazing. Masses of red poppies grow wild everywhere as well as a tall Queen Anne's lace look-alike.

The mechanisms to operate the locks vary widely—some have wooden balance beams while others have iron rods—and there are different procedures for winding up the paddles or sluice gates to close the locks. This diversity is sometimes attributed to the Resistance movement efforts during World War II to confuse the occupation troops and block transportation. Many of the locks we passed through were operated by hard-working women whose menfolk were probably out on their jobs. Often you will see vegetables, flowers, eggs, or wine offered for sale as a means of supplementing meager lockkeeper incomes. Although there seemed to be a preponderance of elderly lockkeepers, younger people are now being lured to this simple bucolic life. This trend may save the tradition of the hardworking lockkeeping family from extinction. In some instances the lockkeeper tends only one lock, but occasionally he or she will tend two, driving back and forth between them. With few exceptions, the people we encountered were friendly and obliging. One hard and fast rule we learned, however, is that the lockkeeper's lunch hour is absolutely inviolable and can last for up to two hours!

This day, while waiting for a lock to open, we tied up on the canal bank for our onboard picnic. A woman drove up to our mooring in a small van stocked with a variety of home-baked breads and a local specialty, *gougères* or puffy cheese balls, also called *Pets de Nonne*. We bought enough of these cheese concoctions to go around to our crew. They made such a huge hit that we had them almost every day afterwards, buying them in village shops. In France they are usually served as a first course. No matter how large a quantity we brought on board, they seemed to vanish in no time.

 Gougères
(Makes about one dozen)

1¼ cups sterilized milk
½ stick butter
1 teaspoon salt

freshly ground black pepper
pinch of cayenne pepper
freshly grated nutmeg (to taste)
1 cup flour
4 eggs
1 cup Gruyère cheese, diced

If not using sterilized milk, bring to boil, and take off skin that forms. Otherwise, add butter in little pieces and bring to boil. Add seasonings, and continue to boil until milk and butter have blended together. Reduce heat and add sifted flour all at once. Stir energetically with a wooden spatula until the paste comes away from sides of the pan.

Remove from heat, and add eggs one at a time. Stir well after each addition, and make sure each is thoroughly incorporated before adding the next. Add diced cheese (reserving a few cubes) and mix well.

Butter a baking tray and arrange 1 tablespoon of the paste at even intervals. Place reserved cheese on top of each mound and brush with a little milk. Cook for about 45 minutes in a moderate to hot oven, without opening door. Serve either hot or cold. (If served hot, prick to release steam.)

In mid-afternoon we passed the dramatic limestone cliffs of Le Saus-sois, a rock face used by climbers as a challenging practice ground.

Châtel-Censoir

Our destination today was the village of Châtel-Censoir which, despite its small size (population 677), had a good range of amenities. The village occupies the side of a steep hill on the summit of which is St.-Potentien Collegiate Church. After an uneventful day on the canal we tied up at the little marina below the town. To stretch our legs, visit the church, and enjoy the view from the summit, Tom, Sue, and I hiked up the hill with a certain amount of huffing and puffing. We had read in the Michelin guide that the Romanesque church choir dated back to the eleventh century while the nave and aisles are sixteenth century. The choir is over an even older crypt containing some ancient unfinished capitals. The view from the top alone was well worth the hike, and the way down was a lot easier on the legs.

That night we walked to the only restaurant in town, L'Etape des Gourmets. Dining outside in a walled garden, we enjoyed a simple but delicious dinner. That evening Sue began reading to the girls from *The*

Penny Dreadfuls, a collection of stories her father had written about the imagined escapades of Sue and her brother Tony on their Long Island farm. Sue's and Tony's plots to make trouble for the crotchety farmer, though they seem rather tame by today's standards, captivated the girls who insisted on nightly readings afterwards.

The chef of L'Etape, Dominique Moreau, sent us a favorite recipe which Sue has adopted as follows:

 Eggs with Sauce Meurette
Serves four

8 eggs
¼ pound smoked pork (smoked turkey breast or ham could be substituted)
1 root parsley (a root vegetable common in Europe, rare in the United States; if unavailable, substitute a small parsnip root)
¼ pound mushrooms
3 cups Burgundy or similar red wine
8 slices toasted country bread

Finely chop the pork, mushrooms, and the parsley (parsnip). Sauté with a tablespoon or so of butter in a quart saucepan until lightly browned. Deglaze with the wine. Season with salt and pepper and boil gently for 20 minutes. To slightly thicken the sauce stir in a teaspoon-sized lump of *beurre manié* (butter mixed with an equal amount of flour).

Poach the eggs (adding a few drops of vinegar to the water). Drain them well and place each on a slice of toast. Dress with the sauce.

Chef Moreau suggests this dish as a first course or as a light entrée accompanied by a green salad.

Day 5, Châtel-Censoir to Clamecy (Floating Logs Downstream to Paris)

Early morning fog gave way to bright sun, and we soon passed through the first of the ten locks we would encounter today. These would include our first self-service lock, number 49, where a sign posted at lockside explained how the mechanism works. More verdant fields with cattle grazing, more forest areas with more song birds, and in the distance at one point a huge walled chateau. Our goal for the lunch stop was Pousseaux, selected because of the amenities, including showers in a public bathhouse, shown in the *Guide Vagnon*. After lunch I headed for the shower, while everyone else decided to go shopping. No interest was shown in either the prehistoric cave or the nineteenth-century church cited in our literature. The girls were especially keen to replenish the depleted stock of Evian, but the store in Pousseaux was closed. The nearest other grocery was reported to be in Surgy, about one and a half kilometers away on the opposite side of the canal. When they found that grocery store, however, it too was closed, and they had to return empty-handed from this wild goose chase, what the French call *cherchant midi à quatorze heures.*

Four more locks in the afternoon and we arrived in the port of Clamecy (population nearly 6,000). Although much smaller than Auxerre, Clamecy shares some of its architectural and topographical charm. Old houses line winding streets leading from the waterfront to the uphill town center. Moreover, both towns were prominent in the practice of collecting logs and floating them down river to Paris, an enterprise dating back to the sixteenth century. Typically the Clamecy timbermen would cut down trees in the Morvan Forest, stack the trimmed logs along the banks of rivers flowing into Clamecy, and mark each log with its owner's name. A dam would be built at Clamecy to collect the logs, and timbermen would harpoon the logs and form them into huge rafts sometimes measuring as much as 7,000 cubic feet. In mid-March at floodwater time, the dam would be breached so that these huge rafts could float downstream passing Auxerre and on to Paris. Each year in early spring some 70,000 tons of timber would float down river for a period of about nine days. This *flottage* traffic continued until 1927, often causing serious delays to normal barge traffic.

A room displaying the history of *flottage* is one of several exhibitions in a museum dedicated to the writer/philosopher Romain Rolland, a native of Clamecy. On the waterfront stands a bronze statue to Jean Rouvet, a pioneer in this industry in 1549.

Walking About in Clamecy

We visited St. Martin's Collegiate Church built between the twelfth and sixteenth centuries, a structure remarkable for the flamboyant

decoration of its high tower contrasting with the austerity of the rest
of the building. A modern church built in the round, which intrigued
us on our walk, was dedicated to Our Lady of Bethlehem. This church
commemorates a succession of fifty bishops of Bethlehem who began
taking refuge in Clamecy after a twelfth-century crusader, who died of
the plague in Palestine, had deeded one of his estates for the bishops' protection.

Always on the lookout for promising restaurants, we spotted the
Hostellerie de la Poste, where we made a reservation for dinner. Kate
and Perrin each ordered *escargots,* a new culinary adventure for them

which to our surprise they relished. Julia discovered the delights of a *soufflé au chocolat*. Except for the slow service, this dinner was very enjoyable.

Day 6, Clamecy to Cuzy

As usual, Tom made certain that the *Matisse* was the first barge under way and the only one in our first lock. We were often the only barge at a lock, but we also had the company of other boats from time to time. In addition to three or four barges operated by Americans, we encountered Belgians, English, Germans, and even one French couple. It strikes us as odd that the French, who love outdoor recreation and have such lengthy vacation time prescribed by law, seem almost oblivious to the attraction of barging on their own waterways. The French couple, who followed us through several locks, were always in some kind of dire straits, rushing about and shouting at each other. Once, when the lock had filled and they were trying to get under way, they did not realize that their stern line was still looped around a bollard until Julia spotted the problem and freed the line for them.

This afternoon, while I was working on some sketches, the others took off in search of a grocery store and post office in Tannay, one and a half kilometers away. They anticipated an easy ride on gentle slopes. But the road turned out to be a long continuous climb, so long that Sue, falling well behind the other bikers, had to dismount and walk. A woman hanging out laundry in her yard casually informed her that the downhill ride would be more enjoyable. Sue then had the satisfaction of seeing the others up ahead dismount, still well short of the town. Once at the top everyone collapsed at an outdoor café table for cool drinks and contemplation of the easy ride down.

Back on board the *Matisse*, Sue wanted to write in her diary but couldn't find it. She searched the entire barge and asked everyone to check their cabins. Much to my embarrassment, the diary turned up the next day in my paint box. To this day I can't figure out who put it there!

That evening we dined outdoors at the Hotel-Restaurant du Morvan in Cuzy. Other bargers were sitting at adjoining tables. M. *le Patron* turned out to be a trumpet player who enjoyed serenading his guests.

Day 7, Cuzy to Chitry-les-Mines (the Final Stretch)

On the last leg of our trip we had ten locks to pass through and three manually operated drawbridges to go under—a new experience, but quite easy to handle. Since lunch on board was to be our last meal, frugal Sue displayed her mastery of the fine art of using up. Her diary notes that we used up leftover cheese, bread, and fruit. To supplement low rations, we bought a baguette and fruit tarts from a van which conveniently came by our mooring.

Tom had adhered so carefully to his timeline that we arrived at the Rive de France marina in Chitry-les-Mines in mid-afternoon, with time to spare. After a fruitless search for a post office for mailing postcards, the rest of the afternoon was passed with biking, reading, and loafing. We found that the nearest restaurant was in Corbigny, and it required two taxis to take us there for dinner. We dined at the outdoor tables of Restaurant le Marode attached to the Hôtel La Buissonnière where we enjoyed one of the best dinners of the week. Unfortunately we were unable to obtain a recipe from this restaurant.

A memorable aspect of this evening was a small ceremony that took place at the war memorial on the town square we were facing. Such memorials, found almost universally in French towns and villages, are dedicated to soldiers killed in World War I, with the names of victims of World War II inscribed on a separate plaque. This particular evening there was a small contingent of elderly veterans, each carrying the *Tricolore*, standing in front of the memorial. A younger man was addressing them over a microphone. Sue and I went over to listen to him but could not quite make out the thrust of his remarks. Finally we realized that this was June 18, the anniversary of General De Gaulle's radio address from London urging on the French Resistance movement and promising his return to drive out the occupying German forces. The speech was a reading of those inspiring words, and as we listened we could understand why they are repeated all across France every year.

Day 8, Chitry-les-Mines *(Adieu Matisse)*

One last breakfast on board, final packing, and making way for the Rive de France cleanup crew to prepare the *Matisse* for its next charter. Two other barges were going through the same process—Rive de France hands scrubbing down decks, cleaning cabins, and checking off all the safety and comfort items belonging to the barge. Fresh linens and towels were installed, galley and heads washed thoroughly. The routine for charter turnover seemed to be well established, and all went smoothly. I went to the marina office to pay for the fuel we had used during the week.

The van from Paris arrived on schedule, and we loaded all our luggage into it. We said goodbye to the *Matisse* with mixed emotions—sadness to see our week on board come to an end, satisfaction at having fulfilled a mission, and eagerness to reach our next destination, Paris. We had worked together as a team and as a family covering the vast distance of 100 kilometers in one week. We knew that the experience would remain in our collective memories for many years to come. The promise of Paris, coming so hard upon the end of our journey, added a joyful note to the more somber aspect of departure. *Adieu Matisse—Bonjour Paris!*

THREE

The Cuisines of Burgundy

A Rich Diversity

Because Burgundy encompasses such a variety of geographical areas, all of which have been exposed to different culinary influences over the centuries, we must recognize that no such thing as a single Burgundian cuisine exists. Different parts of the region have different styles of cooking, so a discourse on the joys of eating in Burgundy should celebrate the variety of choices. Generalizations about "Burgundian cuisine" are unreliable. Perhaps the most common of such observations is that food in this region is hearty, served in substantial portions for lusty gourmand appetites, and based on earthy ingredients found in a peasant's fare, *cuisine bourgeoise*. Burgundians are sometimes referred to as "trenchermen."

While there is some truth in these notions, they could also apply to several other areas of France. Moreover, they miss the point that Burgundy boasts four of the fifteen three-star restaurants listed by Michelin outside of Paris, as well as a host of other well-ranked restaurants offering sophisticated fare. Food critic Waverly Root claims that no other area of France, even the Ile-de-France, has such a high level of good eating throughout its territory. Nothing matters more regarding the culinary standards of a region than the quality of the local ingredients. Burgundy has the rare distinction of excelling in three: beef, mustard, and wine.

Burgundy Beef

In food circles all over the world, the first item considered to represent the food of Burgundy is *boeuf bourgignon,* a beef dish cooked in red wine sauce typically with mushrooms, tiny onions, and bits of bacon. The beef for which Burgundy is renowned comes from Charolais steers, the striking off-white beasts bred originally in the region of Charolles. Originating in the stretch of land east of the Saône from Dijon down

to Mâcon in southern Burgundy, these cattle are now raised in many parts of the world.

Normandy produces more of this breed than Burgundy, but the latter's stock are considered superior in quality—more flavorful and tender. Charolais are also produced in the rugged forests of the Morvan district and in the Nivernais to the north of Charolles, and this beef-oriented territory comprises one of the several culinary centers of Burgundy. Elsewhere in Burgundy one sees fine specimens of milk cows such as the brown Swiss which contribute to the thriving dairy and cheese industry.

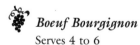

Boeuf Bourgignon
Serves 4 to 6

This beef stew is a classic Burgundian dish for which there are countless recipes developed by chefs around the world over the centuries. The following is a generic recipe to be altered by cooks wishing to improvise according to their own tastes.

2 pounds lean stewing beef cut into 1½ in. cubes

3 tablespoons butter

1 tablespoon flour

1½ cups Burgundy or comparable dry red wine

2 onions, coarsely chopped

1 large carrot cut into pieces

2 shallots, minced

1 large clove garlic, minced

1 bouquet garni (or chopped fresh rosemary, thyme, or other herb)

1 tablespoon Brandy

2 tablespoons Madeira wine

½ pound raw mushroom caps

parsley for garnishing

In a heavy oven-proof casserole, brown beef in 2 tablespoons of butter. Sprinkle with the flour; add salt and pepper and the wine. In separate pan, brown onions in 1 tablespoon of butter. Add to the meat along with the cut-up carrot, garlic, shallots, and bouquet garni or other herb. Add water just to cover. Put the lid on and simmer for 3 hours or until meat is very tender and sauce a rich dark brown. Half an hour before serving, add the brandy and Madeira and the mushroom caps. Sprinkle with chopped parsley. Serve with mashed potatoes or buttered rice.

Cheeses

With so many herds of world-class cattle it is not surprising that Burgundy produces a variety of great cheeses. Epoisses, which had been recommended to Sue and me by our Parisian friend, Sylvie, and which we located on one of our tours in the village of the same name, is a very pungent cheese with an orange-colored rind sprinkled with the local spirit, Marc de Bourgogne. When ripe, it tends to be quite runny. Similar to Epoisses but a bit spicier is Langres, a soft cheese also featured on many Burgundy cheese trays. St. Florentin, another strong, sharp cheese produced in the region around the town of that name, was one of the first we sampled from the impressive cheese tray in our hotel in St. Florentin at the start of our barge trip.

Burgundy cheese trays always feature cheeses made from local goats' milk. These animals cavort about in domestic farmyards and wilder

places, feasting on whatever edibles nature or the goat keeper provides. Goats thrive especially in the rugged terrain of the Morvan forest, and that area accounts for a big segment of Burgundy's goat cheese production. One of the most popular of these cheeses is Montrachet, which is wrapped in chestnut or grape leaves and aged until ripe in cool cellars. A good Montrachet sports a blue rind and a slightly moist interior. The red Burgundies make the perfect complement for all of the cheeses.

Les escargots

Another dish commonly associated with Burgundy is *escargots de Bour-gogne,* snails that are fed royally on select grape leaves on snail farms. Though some evidence suggests snails were consumed in the Neolithic era, the Romans were the first to create recipes for snails, which they fattened with wine and bran. Snails remained popular up until the Middle Ages and were often eaten during Lent.

In the days of the great dukes of Burgundy, snails again came to play a major role in Burgundian fare. In those days the peasants were forced to send the best beef and other produce to the ducal palace in Dijon for the many great banquets staged to impress the dukes' guests. Bereft of their own beef, the farmers had to resort to eating the huge snails that fed on their grape vines. But after being cleaned and boiled, these creatures had very little taste, so they needed a zesty sauce. Thus was born the fabulous mix of butter, garlic, parsley, and shallots, later enhanced by various chefs with many other ingredients to glorify the lowly snail. Now, though the cult of the snail has spread around the globe, they are still regarded as a special delicacy, and non-French children tend to look askance at them. Thus, as noted above, Sue and I were delighted when our granddaughters dared to choose snails at a restaurant we visited on our barging trip.

Today there are two main types of snails in France, of which the Burgundian variety, *Helix pomatia*, is the best known. It has a pretty tan shell with brown spirals and is larger than the *petit gris* found to the west in Charente and the south in Provence and Languedoc. The Burgundian variety, though considered more tender and finer in the quality of its flesh, has the disadvantage of being more difficult to cultivate and is thus more generally harvested in the wild. The *petit gris* is easily raised and thus more readily available in the marketplace, but their production still falls short of meeting demand.

Outside of France devotees of snails go to great lengths to procure and prepare this delicacy. Snails are exported from France in several forms, including canned snails usually with a separate package of shells which can be reused, and frozen snails either in their shells or in a puff pastry. For serious cooks not content to serve prepackaged dishes, the closest approximation to Burgundian *escargots* would be to follow this recipe using the canned snails. A few snail farms in the United States cater mainly to restaurants. Essential equipment for serving snails consists of snail dishes (usually metal), shell-shaped clamps, and small two-pronged forks. A first course of snails usually provides six snails per person. A dozen would be offered for a main course. This is a recipe for the garlic butter sauce for four first-course servings. The snails can be prepared in advance, chilled, and heated before serving.

 Escargots de Bourgogne

    3 ounces of butter
    ¼ cup of minced parsley
    4–5 minced and crushed garlic cloves
    2–3 minced shallots
    pinch of nutmeg
    pepper and salt to taste

Cream these ingredients together for the garlic butter sauce. Drain the brine from the snails, place one in each shell, and pack each shell with the garlic butter sauce. Arrange snails with open ends up in the snail dishes and heat in a 450 degree oven until they are bubbling hot. Serve in same dishes along with plenty of French bread for soaking up sauce.

Wine sauces *(meurettes)*

Since Appendix A deals in greater detail with Burgundian wines, we will not treat wine here except for its use in food preparation. Perhaps the oldest and best-established convention in Western culinary circles is the meat and red wine combination. Various parts of Burgundy have developed a multitude of recipes for cooking beef in red wine, sauces that Burgundians call *meurettes*. These sauces, usually well spiced and thickened with flour, butter, or cream, can accompany not only meat such as beef but also fish, eggs, or certain wild fowl dishes. Burgundy is well endowed with local ingredients aside from beef cattle to add diversity to the table. For example, near Charolles, the area of Bresse is the home of the succulent *poularde de Bresse,* a breed of chicken so prized that the breeders have established an *appellation d'origine contrôlée* comparable to those that guard the quality standards of the best wines and cheeses. From pork raised all over Burgundy comes a well-known *jambon persillée,* a terrine of coarsely chopped ham set in a green wine-flavored parsley and garlic gelatin. The waters of the Seine yield a wide variety of fish including pike, perch, tench, and river eel. One of the traditional Burgundy dishes, *pochouse,* is a stew made up of a mix of all the river fish cooked in wine sauce.

Although pike has a delicious flavor, it is a bony fish, not easy to eat. The Burgundians found an ingenious solution to this problem by conceiving the *quenelle,* a mash of the pike strained through a sieve, mixed with egg whites and *crème fraiche,* and poached in a stock with a white wine. Another triumph of culinary inventiveness! The white wine of choice for fish dishes is Chablis, best-known of the Burgundian whites produced on vineyards in the Yonne centering on the town of Chablis.

Mustard

The history of Burgundy mustard stretches back to the Romans who brought the seeds to Gaul in the days of empire. Even before the Romans, ancient civilizations had held the mustard plant in high regard, believing that the taste of mustard flavoring was good and also good for you. The Roman seeds flourished in the soil and climate of their new home to the point that mustard flavoring gained wide acceptance. Ninth-century French monasteries were receiving handsome returns from their mustard preparations. By the fifteenth century a mustard-makers guild had been formed in Dijon, which became the premier mustard-producing region in France and indeed the foremost area on the globe. About half of all the mustard produced in France comes from Dijon, and it is widely acclaimed as the superior type. The tart taste of Dijon mustard stems from dissolving the mustard seed flour either in white wine or the juice of unripe grapes. A staple in dishes calling for mustard, Dijon is used to a lesser degree as a condiment by itself. One of Sue's tried and true recipes is a mustard sauce which she has refined over the years.

 Sauce rémoulade

A basic formula for this sauce follows:

1 cup mayonnaise
2 tablespoons Dijon mustard
1 tablespoon drained and chopped capers
1 tablespoon chopped cornichons or cucumber pickles
½ teaspoon anchovy paste
finely chopped parsley, tarragon, or chives to taste

Often served with cold meat, poultry, or lobster, this sauce is also featured in celery root rémoulade (julienned celery root mixed with the sauce). There are a zillion recipes for this sauce, all slightly different. The foundation is mayonnaise into which is mixed Dijon mustard, chopped capers and cornichons, anchovy paste, chopped parsley, tarragon, or chives. A simplified rémoulade consists of just the mayo, capers, and Dijon mustard, but adding all or some of the other ingredients gives a tangier taste. You can use store-bought mayo, but if you chose to make your own, the sauce can be made at the same time.

While today we take mustard pretty much for granted as an essential in every cook's kitchen, over the centuries mustard was an obsession shared by the well-born and the commoner. King Louis XI, who was always afraid of being poisoned, took along a jar of his own blend of mustard on his travels near and far. The great dukes of Burgundy in pursuing their many military exploits always made sure the supply wagons were well stocked with *moutarde de Dijon*. In the eighteenth and nineteenth centuries many ordinary households in Paris and most other French cities replenished their mustard pots daily with fresh mustard from special mustard shops in the same manner that they acquired fresh bread or coffee beans. The mustard shops offered nearly a hundred different varieties of mustard seasoning based on a range of ingredients including anchovies, garlic, truffles, and edible flowers such as nasturtiums and roses. But Dijon has always been recognized as the supreme mustard center.

In 1390 Dijon passed its first city ordinance prescribing how Dijon mustard should be made. The strict recipe has been maintained with little change up until today. It calls for black or brown mustard (stronger than the white) ground and passed through a sieve. Mixing with white wine from unripened grapes produces the well-known light yellow paste. In 1870 Maurice Grey and Auguste Poupon opened a mustard shop still in business at 32 rue de la Liberté, the main shopping street in Dijon and still offering an assortment of mustards in beautiful hand-painted porcelain jars now popular with the tourist trade. The Maille brand, even older than Grey-Poupon, is widely distributed in the United States. Beaune, competing for the tourist dollar, has also become a major purveyor of mustard sauces. Bordeaux is the second largest producer of mustard after Burgundy, and French mustard altogether accounts for 47 percent of all European prepared mustard.

The French have always had a preference for the strong pungent mustard traditionally associated with Dijon. French mustard fanciers look askance at some of the far-out mustard mixes now being avidly consumed outside of France especially in the United States—aromatic mustards featuring such exotics as ginger, peanut, or pineapple and, instead of unripened white wine, gin, whiskey, or cognac. However, mustard producers, mindful of the value of exporting their product, have given in to some extent and are now bringing out new flavors for the "benighted" foreign trade.

While the mustard produced from the Dijon region was traditionally made from local mustard seed, farmers have found that they can earn more from producing a cousin of mustard, rapeseed, which closely resembles mustard growing in the field. Rapeseed oil, used as a lubricant, has a strong market in Europe. Now Dijon and all other French mustard makers import their seed from western Canada. Thus one more centuries-old agricultural tradition has yielded to the forces of a global economy.

The Gastronomic Divisions of Burgundy

As noted at the beginning of this chapter, a traveler through Burgundy encounters several different cuisines determined in part by the topography, climate, and soil for nurturing local produce and in part by culinary traditions. Burgundy cuisines remain stoutly faithful to these traditions. As one authority has observed, the attitude of Burgundy is antithetical to culinary fashion. Nevertheless, just as Burgundy cuisines have heavily influenced those beyond its borders, so outside influences creep into Burgundy with a Burgundian twist. In the absence of an ideal logic for dividing the various gastronomies of Burgundy, our discussion will be based on each of the four departments of Burgundy—Yonne, Côte d'Or, Saône-et-Loire, and Nièvre. Gastronomy in each department is influenced to some extent by the cuisines of its neighbors.

Department of Yonne

Because the Yonne was the department in which most of our barge trip took place and since it is closest to Ile-de-France, where much of the best in French cuisine is concentrated, we will begin with that department. Sue's and my initial exposure to this part of Burgundy was our first barge trip in 1984 from Auxerre to Montbard. That trip began our sixteen-year love affair with France. An attractive young French-woman in a van went along with the barge shopping for morning *croissants* and other grocery needs and also took us on sightseeing and restaurant outings. One day we were supposed to have lunch at the three-star Hostellerie de la Poste in Avallon, only recently revived after

BURGUNDY

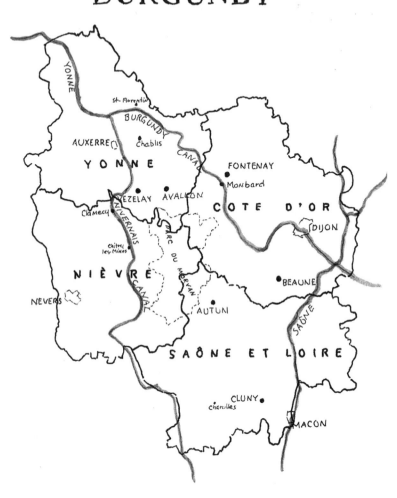

having been closed for a few years but now without the three stars. On our first visit we were captivated by the ambiance of this old establishment, built on two sides of a long courtyard where stage coaches delivered their passengers in days gone by. The bedrooms of the inn were situated in two balconied wings flanking the courtyard. We could sense from the decor of the dining room, with its tables set with fine china and linen, and the stylish clientele that we were in for a great gastronomic experience. But, sad to say, there had been some mix-up in our reservation, and we were turned away. Our substitute venue for lunch involved a drive of some distance over a lovely winding road to the Hôtel Restaurant Moulin des Ruats with a garden on a murmuring stream in the Vallé du Cousin. We were entirely content with this attractive fallback, but having missed out on the Hostellerie de la Poste rankled a bit, and we vowed to come back another time on our own with a confirmed reservation.

Thus two years later we found ourselves driving a little Renault Elf from Paris to Avallon with a reservation for an overnight stay in the place that had turned us away. We arrived around midday to find that our room was not yet ready for occupancy. Now we know never to expect a room anywhere in France until mid-afternoon. Foiled once again, we took off in our car hoping to revisit nearby Vézelay but with no idea of where we might have lunch. This is when Fate dealt us an incredible favor.

L'Espérance   As we were approaching Vézelay, I spotted an impressive collection of handsome automobiles parked near an elegant iron-grill gate opening to an imposing hotel and restaurant. A large sign proclaimed *L'ESPERANCE!* We had stumbled on one of the great restaurants of France, but hardly dared hope that we could be served lunch without a reservation. But, amazingly enough, the *Mâitre d'* found us a table on a terrace overlooking the garden just beyond the main dining area, which is enclosed in a kind of greenhouse.

The story of L'Espérance and its founder-chef, Marc Meneau, is one of the great tales of contemporary culinary entrepreneurship. Meneau followed an unusual route to his pinnacle of success. A native of Vézelay, he chose not to wander far afield to serve an apprenticeship with a known master chef. Instead he essentially taught himself not only to become a great chef but also how to succeed in the competitive restaurant business. Not long after he opened his establishment, his genius was recognized by Michelin which, early in his career, awarded him the coveted three-star rank, with three rosettes and the red hotel icon for an *hôtel agréable*. Discriminating gourmet clientele were soon beating

a path to his doors, and Meneau worked hard to please his guests and hold on to his three-star rank.

Not willing to confine his efforts to running the restaurant and hotel, he has branched out in several directions, greatly enlarging the main restaurant with its Plexiglas rooftop, planting vineyards to produce good wines for his tables, co-authoring *Musée Gourmand,* a book illustrated with paintings of food, adding several annexes to the main hotel including a converted mill, and opening a second restaurant, Le Pré des Marguerites (two Michelin forks) in 1992. While some superstar chefs choose to extend their reach by going to different locations for new ventures, Meneau has stuck close to home, becoming the principal industry of his little village, Saint-Père-sous-Vézelay.

After Sue and I lucked into lunch at L'Espérance, she wrote in her diary that the food was "fabulous," the service "excellent," and the prices "expensive." A mixed review in the October 1994 *La Belle France* newsletter, while praising some of the dishes sampled, gave low marks to others, sharply criticized the service, and agreed with Sue's comment on the prices. Patricia Wells in her *Food Lover's Guide* and the *Hachette Guide* have positive reviews of L'Espérance. It ranks as one of the outstanding hotel/restaurants in Burgundy and, indeed, all of France.

We lingered, as the French do, over such a memorable lunch before driving back to Avallon and the Hostellerie de la Poste where our room had been readied and where we were expected for dinner. That was another exceptional dining experience, but Sue's diary mentions only a creamed vegetable soup. The pleasant memory of that evening lingers now entwined with our recollection of l'Espérance.

La Côte St.-Jacques   Above Auxerre in Joigny on the Yonne River is La Côte St.-Jacques, a hotel restaurant complex that has attained a formidable reputation since its humble beginning as a boarding house in 1952. In that year Marie Lorain began taking boarders in the brick house overlooking the Seine. Since then two successive generations of her family have transformed the original eighteenth-century edifice into a charming hotel surrounded by lovely lawns and gardens, serving some of the best fare in all Burgundy. Marie's son Michel first took over as chef, but was soon joined by his son Jean-Michel to make a team whose greatest ambition is the creation of gastronomic delights. Other family members are responsible for various aspects of management such as reception/concierge functions, accounting, and the operation of the wine *cave*. An impressive collection of Chablis wines from nearby vineyards is the dominant feature of this *cave*.

According to Patricia Wells, the father-son team in the kitchen strikes a balance between the father's inclination toward less aggressive or "quiet" dishes and son Jean-Michel's flare for more assertive fare such as a curried salmon favorite and his gazpacho with shrimp and zucchini mousse. The red Michelin cites as specialties Brittany oysters in a seafood terrine and a walnut, endive, and chanterelles combination. The menu changes with the seasons to take advantage of the produce of local farmers.

As one of the *Relais & Chateaux* listings, La Côte St.-Jacques offers what the chain calls the "refined comfort of a magnificent residence" in its twenty rooms and nine suites. Private cooking lessons and boat rides along the river are special attractions.

Department of Côte d'Or
Bordering the Department of Yonne to the east is the department of Côte d'Or and the famed golden hills of Burgundy's great vineyards.

Here are the capital of Burgundy, Dijon, and its rival town, Beaune, each with two one-star restaurants and a considerable variety of other interesting places for dining. While on our advance scouting expedition, Sue and I visited the barge marina in Dijon and stayed for two days in Beaune.

Dijon   As one might expect of the largest town in Burgundy and its departmental capital, Dijon's cuisine features many traditional specialties. We have discussed the important role of Dijon mustard, but mustard is not the whole story. A good way to see how seriously the citizens of Dijon take the procurement of the best ingredients for the kitchen is to visit the colorful market. Farmers from nearby villages bring their produce to the large covered market in the center of town on Tuesdays, Fridays (the busiest day), and Saturdays. In addition to vegetables and fruits, jugged hare, suckling pigs, undressed chickens, and a variety of freshwater fish for the traditional specialty *pochouse* are all being noisily hawked in this lively marketplace. Dijon's numerous restaurant owners and chefs compete vigorously for the freshest produce.

The red Michelin awards single stars to two Dijon restaurants, Thibert and Au Pré aux Clercs. But Patricia Wells sings the praises of Chef Jean-Pierre Billoux who moved the restaurant bearing his name into Dijon from a nearby village in 1986. Wells call his cuisine "original, almost intellectual, but not the least bit contrived." She especially applauds his choice of all the vegetables to make a serious salad. Wells waxes ecstatic about his first-course salad of poached baby vegetables bathed in a delicate vinaigrette. She also praises the exquisite cheese collection from a leading cheese merchant, Simone Porcheret. If you go to the market, you can also take in this fragrant *fromagerie* adjacent to the market square where you will find some of the prize aged cheeses of the region. Another Dijon specialty is gingerbread or *pain d'epice,* widely available in shops, but especially in the Mulot and Petitjean outlets.

Beaune   As noted above, on our 1998 visit Sue and I stayed at the Hôtel De La Poste conveniently located near the center of town and the famous Hospice in Beaune. The first night we dined in the hotel's restaurant, St.-Christophe, a passable but not memorable experience.

On the second evening we enjoyed a significant dining upgrade at Bernard Morillon, a one-star, three-fork restaurant an easy walk from our hotel. I particularly enjoyed one of their specialties, *Pigeonneau rôti* (roast pigeon) *"Souvaroff."* The area near the Hospice has a great variety of mid-level one- and two-fork restaurants that appeared to us to offer good inexpensive dining opportunities.

Hostellerie de Levernois   A short drive east of Beaune is a Michelin two-star, four-red forks country inn in a park-like setting with ponds and an ancient waterwheel. With fourteen rooms, two suites, and a restaurant offering gourmet cuisine, this inn would appeal to tourists seeking a location outside of the bustling town of Beaune but close enough for ready access. Specialties of the restaurant include a casserole of Burgundy *escargots* and a roast of the famous Bresse chicken. More than 800 vintages are maintained in their *cave.*

La Côte d'Or   Another country inn on the western departmental border is La Côte d'Or, both a three Michelin star and a *Relais &*

Chateaux establishment in the town of Saulieu. Under the direction of master chef Bernard Loiseau, La Côte d'Or has won acclaim for its ambiance and its cuisine. In a country setting with overnight accommodations limited to seven rooms and eight suites, this inn bows to the simple rather than the *grand luxe*. Saulieu is in the Morvan Regional Park, a heavily forested mountainous area popular with outdoor sportsmen. Loiseau, still relatively young to have attained his rank in the culinary world, is best known for bringing out the maximum flavor from local produce, especially vegetables and fruits. Even so, both the red Michelin and the review in the *Relais & Chateaux* directory commend a dish featuring free-range chicken dressed with warm *foie gras* and pureed truffles. Another specialty is frogs' legs cooked in a garlic and parsley extract sauce. However, Patricia Wells was quite critical of Loiseau's lean cuisine specialties when he was largely replacing cream sauces with those based on vegetables. She tempered her criticism of the vegetarian dishes by applauding his preparation of frogs' legs.

Like many of the great chefs of France, Bernard Loiseau as entrepreneur has added other restaurants to his Saulieu base. He now operates three Parisian restaurants including Restaurant Tante Marguerite on the rue de Bourgogne next to Sue's and my current favorite, Hôtel Bourgogne et Montana. We happily dined there twice on our last stay in Paris. Not missing a beat when it comes to promotion, M. Loiseau like other chefs has his own web site as noted in Appendix C.

Château de Gilly   North of Beaune on the N74 at Vougeot is the Château de Gilly, a restoration of the old Cistercian abbey of Citeaux, where St.-Bernard began his ministry. Citeaux was founded in 1098 as a breakaway from Cluny Abbey, and the chateau was built in 1551 by the forty-eighth abbot. Although the monks lived in the harsh simplicity required of their order, they took pride in entertaining representatives of the establishment such as bishops and government officials in a palatial environment where they were served elegant dinners and the finest wines from their vineyard, Clos de Vougeot. That vineyard is now the headquarters of the *Confrérie des Chevaliers du Tastevin*.

Founded in 1934 by wine producers as a means of boosting sales during a depression-era slump, this "Brotherhood of Wine Tasting

Knights" bought the chateau of Clos de Vougeot in 1944 as a regal meeting place for their gatherings, called chapters. At some twenty chapters around the world each year, the scarlet and gold-clad officers of the *Confrérie* initiate new members at elaborate banquets. The wines from this vineyard have been highly prized by connoisseurs for centuries. Ironically, when the monastery was active, the poor monks who produced these wines were forbidden by their vows to bring them to their lips. Today's visitors can take advantage of the guided tours and wine tastings offered during the season by Clos de Vougeot.

Although much of Citeaux was destroyed during the French Revolution and the monks were forced to abandon it, in 1798 a group of Trappist monks returned, restored some of the old buildings, and built a new monastery. Their complex is not open to the public, but a small shop offers some of their books, crafts, and Citeaux cheese sold only here.

The old abbey, now converted to a hotel with forty-nine rooms and nine suites, offers guests stately surroundings, elegant decor, high vaulted ceilings, and a palpable sense of the past. Horse-drawn carriage rides through lovely countryside and hot air balloon rides can be arranged.

Not too far to the south on the N74 is Nuits St.-Georges, second only to Beaune as a wine center. Although the town is somewhat lacking in atmosphere, it has a lively and friendly feel. On our last visit Sue and I enjoyed a good people-watching lunch in an outdoor café in the center of town.

Department of Saône-et-Loire

The department of Saône-et-Loire, south of the Côte d'Or, is named for the two major rivers passing through it, the Loire, the longest river in France, heading north and west toward the Atlantic, and the Saône heading south to Lyons where it joins the Rhone. The catch of the wide, lazy Saône includes pike, perch, tench, and river eel, which along with the local wines provide the makings for the *pochouse* stew mentioned above. Along its shores vegetables flourish, especially asparagus and cauliflower.

Lameloise   South of Beaune via the N74 and N6 lies the small industrial town of Chagny whose chief gastronomic claim to fame is the three-star Lameloise. Near the post office on picturesque Place d'Armes is an old house run as an inn by the Lameloise family for over a hundred years. Its seventeen rooms, given top ranking by *Relais & Châteaux,* fully complement the kitchen where Lameloise père and fils perform their wonders. Their specialties, a ravioli of *escargots* in a sweet garlic broth and roasted pigeon in a truffle crumble, draw gourmets from all corners of the globe. The wine list features not only great *grand crus* at the high end but less pricey local vintages as well. Even so, the tab at Lameloise is not light on the pocketbook, and some travelers may prefer another pleasant stopping place nearby, the Hostellerie du Château de Bellecroix, a twelfth to eighteenth century vine-clad inn set in a park off the N6 below Chagny. The Knights of St. John were sheltered by this ancient edifice in days gone by.

Chalon-sur-Saône   The next town below Chagny is Chalon-sur-Saône which has been an important crossroads since the days of Julius

Caesar. From the banks of the river and the Canal du Centre which joins it, you can watch the steady traffic of pleasure boats during the boating season. An International Fair in June is held around a wildfowl and game market. Aside from an area of old half-timbered houses on the pedestrian street by St.-Vincent Cathedral, Chalon's architectural attractions are limited, but it does have a one-star restaurant, St.-Georges, convenient to the bus and train stations.

Mâcon Mâcon is the largest town in the southern tip of the Saône-et-Loire department. A hotbed of Protestantism during the pre-Revolutionary era, it was at odds with the Catholic Dukes of Burgundy who never brought the splendors of their court here. During the Revolution the people of Mâcon destroyed the nearby Abbey of Cluny and eleven other churches, so that the modern town is bereft of the ancient ecclesiastical landmarks that lend character to other towns and cities of Burgundy. However, the bustling waterfront with many terrace cafés and restaurants offers today's visitors a pleasing prospect.

Of course, the town is best known as the center of the Mâconais wine business and, among the wine merchants, as the site of the annual French National Wine Fair. Dealers from all over France congregate here every year with their hopes pinned on winning an award allowing them to place a gold and red prize label on their bottles of current vintages. Such prize wines are featured on the wine lists of two restaurants not far from Mâcon, the three-star Georges Blanc in Vonnas and the one-star Château d'Igé.

Although the wines of Château d'Igé are among our favorites, Sue and I have yet to visit the actual chateau for which it is named. It was built in 1235 as a fortified castle with feudal turrets and towers. Now ranked with one Michelin star and a *Relais & Châteaux* listing, it offers such traditional dishes as a filet mignon in red wine sauce. Accommodations consist of seven rooms and eight suites.

Nièvre and Morvan Regional Park

The fourth department in Burgundy and probably the least frequented by tourists is Nièvre, encompassing the Nivernais region and the western sector of the Morvan Regional Park. Nevers, near the western departmental border, is the capital. As noted in chapter 2, our barge trip on

the Nivernais canal took us about a third of the way through the beautiful
unspoiled central part of Nièvre.

The borders of the Morvan encompass the mountainous, heavily
forested terrain that sets it so distinctly apart from the plains or gentle
rolling countryside typical of most of Burgundy. With almost no decent
roads, an infertile soil, and an average of 180 days of rain each year,
the Morvan attracted very few visitors over the years. Indeed it became
an object of scorn among its Burgundian neighbors who attach great
value to the fecundity of land. Only in recent years when the Morvan
has been discovered as an ideal place for outdoor sportsmen has it come
into its own. Now it is a haven for hikers, mountain climbers, fishermen,
rafters, environmentalists, and the "green" tourist trade who delight in
its wildness.

As illustrated by the map, the borders of the Morvan extend into
each of Burgundy's four departments, but the section in Nièvre is by
far the largest. The park's outer reaches encompass two of the great
hotel/restaurants, L'Espérance in the Yonne and La Côte d'Or in the

department for which it is named, but they are out of character with the rest of the park which is devoid of large inns, much less grand hotels. The sportsmen and green tourists now coming to the Morvan tend not to be looking for elegant or expensive dining. In the simpler more rustic inns where they stay, there are, however, a number of special dishes of the region worthy of note that can also appear on menus in other places in Nièvre. These include a cold chump end of veal *à la Clamecyçoise;* ham braised in wine and served with cream sauce; *potée Morvandelle* (a thick meat and vegetable soup); *fricasée Morvandelle* (stew of liver, ox tripe, and blood); and *galettes* (open pastry fruit tarts).

Aside from these down-to-earth offerings, the Morvan is of interest gastronomically mainly as an exporter of such highly valued foodstuffs as snails, mushrooms, fish from its wild rivers, and cheeses, both goat and cow.

Elsewhere in Nièvre there are few restaurants that have received attention from Michelin or other culinary authorities. Chapter 2 cited the various restaurants where we dined on the Nivernais leg of our barge trip, each of which we enjoyed though none are mentioned in the red Michelin. In Nevers, the capital, one restaurant, Jean-Michel Couron, receives a single star. As we have seen, the other three departments of Burgundy offer the gourmet traveler a wide choice of inviting hotels and restaurants for all kinds of dining. Nièvre's attractions are more in the sphere of the Morvan's natural wonders and the simpler fare of a rural area.

FOUR 🍇
In Retrospect

A poem by Colette translated by Sue is one of the best ways I know to evoke the spirit of Burgundy. Colette, who lived from 1873 to 1954, was born in *Saint-Sauveur-en-Puisaye* in the Yonne. This is an extract from *"Les Vrilles de la Vigne,"* The Tendrils of the Vine.

> The perfume of the woods of my childhood's land
> rivals the scent of strawberry or rose
> you would swear
> in summer when the blackberry thicket blooms
> that a fragrant fruit was ripening somewhere
> there   here   quite close by.
> You would swear
> when autumn comes to darken the fallen leaves
> that an apple, overripe, had dropped to earth;
> inhaling the scent, you seek to trace the source
> here   there   quite close by.

Colette's lines dwell on the power of scent to bring back the memory of a place. Indeed, as one walks or rides along the banks of Burgundy's waterways, passing by meadows and under the overarching trees, the scents of the earth and everything growing in it are almost overpowering. Together with the beauty of the natural vistas and the songs of the birds living under the forest canopies, the senses are almost overloaded. As if this were not enough, the sense of taste seems to be sharpened in this environment so that picnics along your barge route or meals in the village restaurants seem to acquire a special piquancy. Almost every wine has something good to say for itself. On the *Matisse* we often commented that "life doesn't get any better than this."

Looking back on that trip now reminds me of the restorative powers of the barging experience. Water Rat's wise words to Mole now sound wiser than ever: "There really is nothing half so much worth doing as simply messing about in boats." Our family spent seven lovely days and nights together not doing a whole lot, mostly watching the peaceful landscape slowly pass by, polishing our routine for negotiating the locks, engaging in a bit of casual sightseeing from time to time, wining and dining with gusto on board the *Matisse* or in village restaurants, star-gazing at night, and chatting with each other about whatever came to mind, trivial or profound. It would be hard to imagine a better therapy for anyone stressed out by the pressures of our dot.com age.

Looking back prompts me to offer two pieces of advice for potential bargers:

1. Don't even consider going on a diet while traveling in Burgundy. If you must, diet before or after Burgundy but not while there. Whether you are on a bare barge or a hotel barge, don't miss out on the hearty character of Burgundy cuisines. Give your taste buds free rein. Maybe by drinking some of the Burgundy red wines you can make the *Paradoxe Français* work for you. But your time in Burgundy is too precious to ruin it by dieting.
2. Don't take your laptop with you. The lackadaisical pleasures of barging cannot be fully enjoyed if they are interrupted by emailing the office, surfing on the Internet, or other distracting computer tasks. Look backwards in time, immersing yourself in the history of this land and the beauty of the landscape, while letting go of your everyday preoccupations for the duration of your cruise.

Barging offers plenty of time for reading. It just makes sense to be reading about Burgundy when you are traveling through it. Find out why the Burgundians are so proud of their heritage and why their ancestors so vigorously struggled to maintain the region's distinctive character. As noted above, before you start out on your cruise you should do some background reading, and you should take a book or two with you when you finally board your barge.

For me the easygoing adventure of the week's barge trip was a prelude to the challenging enterprise of writing this book. Without the

luxury of time to steep myself in the various subjects being treated, I found myself working toward a tight deadline for a final manuscript. There is a wealth of literature on each of these subjects, and I had time to delve into too little of it. Once again, as in the acknowledgments, I must make a bow to all the authorities on Burgundy whose writings I relied on so heavily to bring this book into print.

APPENDIX A 🍇
The Wines of Burgundy

"The only good reason I can think of for going to France is to drink Burgundy in its own land."

Erasmus, 1466–1536

My Epicurean namesake was perhaps the most traveled man of his age, and he had a reputation as a connoisseur of food and wine. His remark on Burgundy wine resonates today. Anyone who goes barging in Burgundy has a golden opportunity, if not an outright obligation, to sample the fruits of the vine for which the region is famed. Whether you are a well-heeled connoisseur interested in the high-end *Grand Crus* wines or a less demanding traveler content to sample more ordinary wines including even those offered for sale at some lockkeepers' houses, the wines of Burgundy will greatly enhance the pleasure of your sojourn. If you can afford the time, days spent before or after your cruise visiting selected wine *caves* will be well rewarded. If your timetable does not permit such a tour, you should make time for some *dégustations* or tastings along your route. Your taste buds will thank you, and your palate will be ennobled.

Burgundy and Bordeaux stand in a class by themselves as great centers of viniculture. But the two regions are very different in many ways. Whereas Burgundy is a landlocked region, lacking a large metropolitan center and known for its hearty country fare, Bordeaux is a thriving port city, one of the most elegant and worldly in all of France, with a refined cuisine to match. The soils and weather conditions are also very different. Still another difference is in the size of landholdings of the growers. In Burgundy the majority of growers are small landholders in some cases owning vineyards of less than ten acres, while in Bordeaux most wine is produced by a few large vintners who constitute a kind of oligarchy.

Vive la différence! Each region grows great grapes making great wines! The growing of grapes in each began in Roman times; during the Middle Ages the monks cultivated their monastery vineyards with care to improve the vine stock. In the intervening centuries, improvement of the grape has become an increasingly serious and complicated enterprise. In fact many people regard French wine classification, nomenclature, and marketing as so arcane and inaccessible that, rather than trying to fathom the technicalities, they simply decide for themselves what wines they like or don't like.

Readers seeking a full comprehension of French viniculture should consult any of the numerous books on the subject, including some of the titles listed in the bibliography. The following brief discussion is what might be called a bare bones primer with a focus on the wines of Burgundy and particularly on those of the Côte d'Or (the Golden Slopes), the department that produces nearly all of the great Burgundian wines.

Grape Varieties

Burgundy produces relatively few wine varieties, of which only four account for the bulk of the harvest. Only rarely are these varieties blended.

Chardonnay

This grape, which is used in the region's best white wines, may actually have originated in Burgundy. There is a town of Chardonnay that might be the birthplace. This wine has now attained worldwide popularity, and many American vineyards feature Chardonnay as one of the principle varieties. The Burgundy version tends to a more earthy or flinty character, whereas many American Chardonnays tend to be riper and more flowery.

Pinot Noir

This is the varietal that produces the greatest red burgundies and the only variety grown in the Côte d'Or. The grape is somewhat temperamental and difficult to grow, hence producing a more expensive wine when it reaches the market. A fine Pinot Noir has a silky texture and a taste reminiscent of dark fruits and game.

Gamay

Beaujolais and the various rosés of the region are made from this red grape. Although Beaujolais is known mainly as a wine to be drunk young, a top of the line Beaujolais can mature well, acquiring a more complex nature and bringing a higher price on the market.

Aligoté

The fourth major variety is grown in the Chablis region in the north of Burgundy and in several other areas of the Côte d'Or. Other varieties grown in smaller quantities include Pinot Blanc and Pinot Gris.

Four Classes of Wine

Côte d'Or wines are divided into four classes. The top class is **Grand Cru,** a category applied to only some thirty-odd vineyards that have the right to sell under the vineyard name without reference to the commune of origin. **Premier Cru,** the second class, including over 300 of the best vineyards, is marketed under the name of the commune followed in the same type size by the name of the relevant vineyard. When a wine is made from more than one vineyard, the label says simply "Premier Cru." The third class, **Village** or **Commune,** covers wines that can be sold with their vineyard names appearing in smaller type beside the name of the village or commune. **Regional** or generic wines made throughout Burgundy such as Bourgogne or Bourgogne Aligoté make up the fourth category.

The Appellation System

The French wine appellation system, like the system for controlling the marketing of more than 400 varieties of cheeses, is characteristic of the French insistence on scientific order and regulation. But for the uninitiated it can be hard to fathom. On the basis of the grape varieties, French law recognizes over 100 different appellations divided into the four classes listed above. Every year sees additional appellations being authorized. The multitude of vineyards and the volume of production in each of the classes in Burgundy further complicate the appellation system here. Whereas the system in general is supposed to help the buyer determine the worth of a bottle, it is of relatively little help in Burgundy. The price of a bottle may have little to do with the quality

LA BOURGOGNE VITICOLE

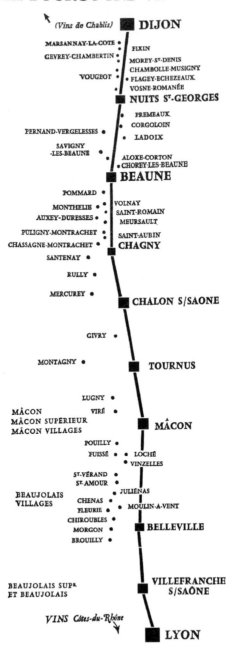

(Vins de Chablis) ■ **DIJON**

MARSANNAY-LA-COTE •
    FIXIN
GEVREY-CHAMBERTIN •
    MOREY-Sᵗ-DENIS
    CHAMBOLLE-MUSIGNY
VOUGEOT •   • FLAGEY-ECHEZEAUX
    VOSNE-ROMANÉE

■ **NUITS Sᵗ-GEORGES**

    PREMEAUX
    CORGOLOIN
PERNAND-VERGELESSES •   LADOIX
SAVIGNY
-LES-BEAUNE •
    ALOXE-CORTON
    • CHOREY-LES-BEAUNE

■ **BEAUNE**

POMMARD •
    VOLNAY
MONTHELIE •   SAINT-ROMAIN
AUXEY-DURESSES •   MEURSAULT
PULIGNY-MONTRACHET •   SAINT-AUBIN
CHASSAGNE-MONTRACHET •   **CHAGNY**
SANTENAY •

RULLY •

MERCUREY •   ■ **CHALON S/SAONE**

GIVRY •

MONTAGNY •   ■ **TOURNUS**

LUGNY •
MÂCON   VIRÉ •
MÂCON SUPÉRIEUR
MÂCON VILLAGES   ■ **MÂCON**

POUILLY •
FUISSÉ •   • LOCHÉ
    • VINZELLES

Sᵗ-VÉRAND •
Sᵗ-AMOUR •
    • JULIÉNAS
BEAUJOLAIS
VILLAGES   CHENAS •
FLEURIE •   • MOULIN-A-VENT
CHIROUBLES •
MORGON •   ■ **BELLEVILLE**
BROUILLY •

BEAUJOLAIS SUPᴸ   **VILLEFRANCHE**
ET BEAUJOLAIS   **S/SAÔNE**

VINS *Côtes-du-Rhône*

■ **LYON**

or the appellation on the label. The quality of wines made by different growers even in the same vineyard can vary greatly due to different winemaking methods, and vintners seem to operate on a philosophy of selling at whatever price the market will bear. The individual buyer therefore must work out the best approach to wine purchasing for his or her own needs. A serious wine lover keeps records of each purchase, grades the wine according to his or her taste, and selects a few favorites for future consideration.

An Embarrassment of Riches

As this graph of *La Bourgogne Viticole* demonstrates, the variety of great Burgundy wines is enough to satisfy the dreams of the most serious connoisseur or to totally confuse the wine neophyte. I happened on this graph in a little restaurant in Vancouver, where the chef took a serious interest in French wines, traveling to France every year to stock his cellar. What better example could there be of the far-flung following of French viniculture? The graph lists the major wines in relation to their respective geographic territories or *terroirs,* literally the soils in which the grapes are grown. The north-south line in the middle of the graph shows the major wine-growing towns or municipalities. Burgundians refer to this line as the Route des Grands Crus starting on the D122 and joining the N74. The Côte d'Or is most often divided in wine parlance between the northern part called the Côte de Nuits after the town Nuits Saint-Georges and the southern part, the Côte de Beaune, named after the town of Beaune. The arrow pointing northwest to *Vins de Chablis* designates the direction of the Chablis region, about 100 kilometers from the Côte d'Or and an entirely different geologic formation. The following discussion will highlight only a select number of the more important wines.

Chablis

The soil of the Chablis region is dominated by limestone which is thought to give the Chardonnay grapes grown there their austere (some say "thin") character. Limestone is also prominent in most Côte d'Or soils but less so than in Chablis. When Sue and I visited the Domaine Laroche *cave* in 1984, Chablis was the most popular white wine being served in America. On our hotel barge trip that year we consumed quite a bit of Chablis. Now its popularity has yielded to other Chardonnays. But on board the *Matisse* last year, in the vicinity of Chablis, we enjoyed a number of Chablis wines, and there were no complaints that they were too thin. There is a great diversity in the wines of this region, ranging from the Grand Cru wines with intense flavors produced on seven northern slopes to those produced in other parts of the region, some of which are disappointing.

The town of Chablis, about fifteen kilometers east of Auxerre, is easily accessible for bargers tied up there. A dozen or more *caves* offer tastings. Because of the extensive damage by World War II bombings and a major tank battle, there are few old streets to visit. But Domaine Laroche has an interesting collection of wine artifacts in a fifteenth-century building on the rue des Moulins. Unlike other wine regions, Chablis has no posted wine routes for visiting vineyards.

Another wine produced in Irancy to the southwest of Chablis, is a red, Bourgogne Irancy, which we tried several times on board the *Matisse* and at restaurants on our route. Because Irancy combines Pinot Noir grapes with a small amount of a local grape César, it is considered superior in body and color to many of the generic reds.

The Great Wines of Côte de Nuits

The majority of Côte de Nuits wines are reds, more robust in character than those of its neighbor to the south. Côte de Beaune, on the other hand, produces all of the great whites of the Côte d'Or as well as many excellent reds. Driving south from Dijon, the first wine center encountered is **Marsannay-la-Côte,** home of the most famous Burgundy rosé. The pinkish color comes from using the last pressings of Pinot Noir grapes, the skins having been removed quickly from the vat. But since the village of Marsannay was granted its own appellation for red and white wines in 1987, the rosé production is being cut back.

Below Marsannay is the town of Fixin, the northernmost of the eight communes of the Côte de Nuits with two Premier Cru vineyards, **Clos de la Perrière,** the best known, and **Clos du Chapître.** These wines have a deep red color, a strong bouquet, and a high alcoholic content. Some experts regard them as rivals of their neighbor to the south, Gevrey-Chambertin. On the highway a large sign boasts of a statue called "The Awakening of Napoleon," showing the great man about to arouse himself from sleep. On a wooded hill above Fixin surrounded by gardens stands a replica of the house where Napoleon lived in exile on St.-Helena.

The municipality of **Gevrey-Chambertin** has the greatest number of Grand Crus vineyards in all of Burgundy, seven in all. A good number of Premier Crus vineyards are located south of the town. The vineyards cover an area of 1250 acres and produce 1,900,000 bottles a year. In 1847 a royal decree granted the town of Gevrey the right to add the illustrious appendage of Chambertin to its official name. This name traces back to a peasant named Bertin of the Middle Ages who copied the methods of the monks in the Cluny abbey of Bèze and produced a wine as good as theirs in his field (or *champ*) thus the name Chambertin. In the village of Gevrey a tenth-century castle with vaulted wine cellars has been restored by the monks of Cluny. The locals of Gevrey proudly claim that Napoleon loved his Chambertin so much that he loaded his wagon train with it for all of his campaigns.

Chapter 3 mentioned the **Clos de Vougeot,** now headquarters for the *Confrérie des Chevaliers du Tastevin.* This famous wine estate dates back some 700 years from its monastic beginnings when the Cistercian monks built a fortified monastery whose walls encompassed fifty acres of vineyards. During the French Revolution when all church property was confiscated by the state, the monk in charge of the cellars, appropriately named Dom Goblet, is reported to have smuggled out enough wine to satisfy himself for a lifetime. Today the vineyard still consists of the same fifty acres, but they are now divided among eighty winegrowers who cultivate some 100 plots. Needless to say, the wines from this vineyard vary greatly in quality, the vines on the top slope being generally considered to produce the better grapes. Next to the Clos de Vougeot is the Premier Cru **Clos Blanc de Vougeot,** producing a fruity white wine. The vineyard complex here attracts many thousands of visitors every year. While tasting of the rarefied Clos de Vougeot is not possible, one can taste some very good Premier Cru wines at Domaine Bertagna near the chateau.

Just below Vougeot is Vosne-Romanée, considered almost hallowed ground by wine connoisseurs. The **Domaine de la Romanée-Conti,** established in 1942, incorporates six Grand Crus vineyards. Recognized the world over for its superb, rich flavor and perfect balance, this wine commands top prices (some would say astronomical) all over the globe. It needs a minimum of ten years to age properly, but the final product is worth the wait.

For over two centuries this vineyard was owned by a family called Croonembourg, and when it was sold in 1760 there were many wealthy contenders bidding for it including Louis XV's greedy mistress, Mme. de Pompadour. She lost out to the Bourbon Prince of Conti, hence the present name of the estate. During the French Revolution, an official document proclaimed this to be the best wine not only in the Côte d'Or but in all of France. Leave it to the French in the middle of a revolution to issue a high-level pronouncement on wine! Another well-known Grand Cru of this estate is La Tâche, a somewhat earthier wine, rather fruity with hints of mushrooms. Some connoisseurs consider this wine to be as good if not better than its more famous neighbor.

The town of Nuits-Saint-Georges is worth a visit as the mercantile center of the region's wine trade. In volume of business it ranks second only to Beaune. Not too much remains in the way of historic atmosphere except around the central Place de la République, a busy intersection with a seventeenth-century clock tower, a handsome church, Saint-Symphorien, and the Hospice Saint-Laurent. Just as in Beaune, hospitals of Nuits have acquired vineyards and benefit from the wine auction held each year on the Sunday before Palm Sunday. On our 1998 scouting trip Sue and I enjoyed a lunch stop here on the main square. We acquired a couple of bottles of one of Nuit's most famous products, **Crème de Cassis,** black currant liqueur used in making Kir.

Kir was an invention of Canon Félix Kir, the mayor of Dijon during and after World War II. Recognizing the sorry state of the local wine growers and the growers of black currants in the postwar depression, he experimented with *blanc-cassis,* a dollop of cassis mixed with a glass of white wine, and decided to serve this as the only apéritif at his official functions. He insisted that the wine be a dry Aligoté, and there is room to doubt that he would have approved of the adaptation, Kir Royale, made with champagne.

Driving south below Premeaux, you reach the town of Corgoloin and a sign marking the boundary between the Côte de Nuits and the Côte de Beaune. A word of clarification about appellations in Beaune is in order here. Wines simply called Beaune are produced on the slopes around the town of Beaune. Wines labeled "Côte de Beaune" come from certain small parcels of land on the Beaune mountain. "Côte de Beaune-Villages" labels signify a blend of two or more red wines from sixteen select villages including some noted below.

In your journey south (real or imaginary) you are now on your way to **Aloxe-Corton,** a typical Burgundian wine working village with a handsome manor house surrounded by vineyards producing the Corton Grand Cru and Premier Cru wines. A legend claims that Emperor Charlemagne had a strong preference for the red wines of Aloxe, but could not prevent them from staining his beard. His mother complained so much that he ordered the vineyard to begin planting white grapes. The Aligoté grape chosen for the replanting would not have made as satisfactory a substitute for the red grape as the more robust Chardonnay which came along much too late for the Emperor. Today Corton Charlemagne is a flinty slow-maturing wine classed among the best of the Burgundy whites. The powerful red Corton also needs plenty of time to mature, but considering the price it commands, it would be foolish to drink it too young. The chateau of Aloxe-Corton is best known for its colored tile roofs in a class with those of the Hospice in Beaune.

To the west of Aloxe Corton, another charming village, **Savigny-lès-Beaume,** is at the entrance to a valley of vineyards producing more red wines than anywhere on the Côte de Beaune. They have the great commercial advantage of maturing fast. A motto written in Latin over the door of the wine cooperative proclaims "There are five reasons for drinking: the arrival of a guest, a thirst, an oncoming thirst, an excellent wine, and any other reason you care to think of."

Next on our itinerary is the town of **Pommard,** center for one of the best-known and full-bodied burgundy reds. These powerful wines have been favorites of such notable figures in history as Henri IV, Louis XV, Victor Hugo, and Thomas Jefferson when he was U.S. Ambassador to France. The Pommards are often served with typical hearty Burgundian dishes such as Boeuf Bourgignon, but their quality can vary tremendously from an unsubtle and tannic character to Premier Crus such as **Les Grands Epinots** or **Les Rugiens,** which are being considered for promotion to Grand Cru status. Pommard is made in the old-fashioned way: the grapes are not stemmed, and they are fermented over a long period.

The wines of Pommard's next-door neighbor to the south, **Volnay,** could hardly be more different. They are delicate, elegant, perfectly balanced, silken red, and ideal accompaniment for a sophisticated and refined cuisine. Louis XI admired this wine so much that, after he had defeated the last Duke of Burgundy, Charles the Bold, he appropriated the entire vintage of 1477 for his own ménage.

Below Pommard and Volnay is the larger town of **Meursault** between the N74 and the D973. The latter, designated the wine route, goes through many of the wine villages and vineyards. If you have plenty of time for wandering, you will be well rewarded by visits to Monthelie, Auxey-Duresses, and Saint-Romain. However, next stop on our selective tour is Meursault, the production center of some of most famous white wines of the Côte d'Or. Ten times more whites than reds are produced here, an unusual ratio in this part of the world. The Château de Meursault cellars, dug by the monks of Citeaux Abbey in the thirteenth century, hold half a million bottles and one thousand oak maturing casks. Visitors may taste wines and walk among the ancient trees in the great park around the chateau. Although no Meursault wines have been granted Grand Cru status, they are considered to be in a class with Montrachet and Puligny, discussed below. Some Meursaults have a flinty dryness, while others are described as evoking hints of cinnamon, sun-drenched fruits, and hazelnuts.

Following the wine route south from Meursault, you come to two villages, **Puligny-Montrachet** and **Chassagne-Montrachet,** each of which decided on the same day in 1879 to add the name Montrachet to its name, honoring the vineyards that had already achieved world-class stature. Wine authorities run out of superlatives in describing these wines; many agree that the Montrachet white is the best anywhere in the world. Alexandre Dumas famously proclaimed that it should be drunk on bended knee with the head bared. There are four Grand Cru Montrachet vineyards—Le Montrachet, Chevalier-Montrachet, Bâtard-Montrachet, and Bienvenues-Bâtard-Montrachet. Connoisseurs insist that this golden liquid be aged for at least ten years and that it be served at cellar (not fridge) temperature. Needless to say, the price levels for these wines assure that they will be treated with reverence by those who serve them. You can taste these wines and decide on making the investment required to buy them at the Château de Puligny-Montrachet. In contrast with Puligny, Chassagne-Montrachet produces mostly red wines although it is a joint owner of two of the Grand Cru vineyards cited above. The Chassagne reds, though not in the same exalted class as the Puligny whites, are still of very high quality and command prices to match.

The town of **Santenay** marks the southern end of the Côte d'Or below which begins the Côte Challonaise. Santenay is actually three small hamlets strung together on the banks of the little river Dheune. Medicinal springs discovered here in Roman times led to the development of a health resort which, because of the idiosyncracies of French law, allowed the town to establish a casino. It's the only one in the Côte d'Or. While the vineyards here used to produce dark, earthy, and beefy wines, modern methods have led to a lighter, fruitier, and more delicate product. A fourteenth-century castle built by the first Duke of Burgundy, Philip the Bold, houses a wine museum. In the Château du Passe-Temps are the largest cellars in the Côte d'Or. Many of the Santenay wines, both red and white, are comparatively reasonable in price and can be tasted in several *caves.*

The western hillside slopes above the Côte d'Or stretching down from Beaune to the area of Santenay are called the **Hautes-Côtes de Beaune.** A drive on back roads through this area takes you to a number of charming small villages surrounded by noticeably less tidy vineyards than those along the Route des Grands Crus. The vines grown here are mainly Aligoté and Gamay, better adapted to the soil and climate at this elevation and more spindly than the Chardonnay and Pinot Noir vines. Near Mercurey one of the more elegant wines is produced in the seventeenth-century Château de Chimirey owned by the Marquis de Jouennes-d'Herville. A visit to his *cave* makes a good goal for a day's excursion.

Even though the **Côte Chalonnaise** is a continuation of the topography of the Côte d'Or, the appearance of the landscape is entirely different. Whereas the latter is almost nothing but one neatly cultivated vineyard after another, the former is a mix of farmyards, fields with cattle, sheep, and goats, woods, and vineyards—a more diverse and, in the eyes of some, a more pleasing prospect. The wines here, less famous and less costly than those of its northern neighbor, are gaining in reputation and represent an attractive value for budget-conscious visitors. In the past most of the Challonais wines have been marketed as generic Burgundies without any reference to specific region, but now there are five appellations for Bouzeron, Rully, Mercurey, Givry, and Montagny. An overall appellation, Bourgogne Côte Challonnaise was created in 1989 to be used on labels for both reds and whites produced in forty-four communes.

Bouzeron is home to an excellent Bourgogne Aligoté now entitled to be sold with the village name on the label. Rully produces aromatic, fresh, and fruity white wines said to have more depth than the reds and a good value. Their sparkling Crémant de Bourgogne is one of the best in Burgundy. The vineyards around Mercurey, the best-known village in the Challonais, are planted 95 percent in red grapes, and the sturdy wines they make are best consumed after aging.

As far back as the sixth century, the wines of Givry were being praised by influential taste setters and wine lovers. They were rated with the wines of Beaune and heavily taxed in Paris. Henri IV, *le Vert Galant,* was said to have loved Givry as much as he loved women, which was a lot. Signs around Givry claim Henri as a patron, and he is featured on the labels of several vintages.

Montagny, marking the southern end of the Challonais, produces a fine white wine comparable to a crisp Pouilly-Fuissé, which was the favorite of the monks of Cluny. Local prices represent a very good value.

The road south from Montagny leads through landscapes similar to the Challonais, a picturesque mix of various agricultural enterprises; and the next great wine region, the **Mâconnais,** blends in almost imperceptibly. One of the signs of change is the appearance of Mediterranean-style red roofs, for you are beginning to cross into a warmer climate zone. Here the grapes ripen earlier than in the rest of Burgundy and the harvest can be a week or two earlier. Although reds were dominant in the past, now the whites are primary, with Chardonnay grapes being cultivated in about two-thirds of the vineyards. The wine labels carry several appellations—Mâcon, Mâcon-Villages, Mâcon followed by a specific village name, or Mâcon Supérieur (containing one percent more alcohol.) The most famous and most expensive wines are produced in the southernmost part of the Mâconnais.

The early recognition of the wines of this region owes much to the initiative of a grower who felt strongly that the Mâcon vintages were not receiving the attention they deserved. Claude Brosse was a giant of a man with great physical prowess and strong convictions. He loaded a couple of hogsheads of his wine on an ox cart and set out for Versailles hoping to persuade some of the courtiers there to start buying Mâcon vintages. After completing the thirty-three-day walk to Versailles, he attended mass to give thanks for his safe journey. King Louis XIV was present and noticed that when all of the congregation was on their knees one man was still standing. Louis sent one of his staff to tell the man to kneel, and found out to his amazement that he *was* kneeling. He then sent for Brosse to find out what had brought him all the way to Versailles. When Louis tasted the wine, he declared it to be superior to what was then being consumed in court. And the rest is history.

The Mâconnais vineyards extend to the south for some fifty kilometers from Tournus on the Saône. A circuitous wine route in the northern sector leads through Chardonnay, the village for which the grape may have been named; Uchizy, home of Mâcon-Uchizy, and Lugny, home of Mâcon-Lugny (two vineyards offering modestly priced wines which have been staples in our house over the years); Viré and Clessé, sources for the appellation Viré-Clessé; and finally leading to the town of Cluny and the ruins of the Benedictine monastery there. As noted in chapter 1, the Cluny monks planted the first grape vines in the area, and, because their vows were less rigid than those of the Cistercians, were able to enjoy the fruits of their labors. Today the grapes grown around Cluny are mainly Chardonnay for whites and Gamay for reds with some Pinot Noir.

The most famous Mâconnais wine is undoubtedly Pouilly-Fuissé, also the most expensive, but not so out of reach as to prevent Sue and me from buying it when there are specials. Its rich, refreshing flavor surpasses many other Burgundy whites. The appellation area for Pouilly-Fuissé lies west of the city of Mâcon in fields dominated by two high rock outcroppings, Solutré and Vergisson, visible at great distances. According to legend, Vercingetorix rallied his troops to fight the Romans by lighting a fire atop Vergisson, and this is remembered today by an annual bonfire on midsummer's day. A Pouilly-Fuissé *cave* in Solutré is an outlet for the local vineyards, and tastings are offered for a fee. Energetic walkers can climb to the top of Solutré.

Some less expensive substitutes for Pouilly-Fuissé include the popular

St. Véran, produced in seven area villages, and two harder-to-find wines, Pouilly-Vincelles and Pouilly-Loché. When shopping in Vincelles on the fourth day of our barge trip, we picked up some of that wine which we enjoyed at picnic lunches on board the *Matisse*.

The town of Mâcon is a busy river port with a population of 40,000. It has been involved in the transport of wine for centuries and now is the site for the French National Wine Fair in the last two weeks of May each year. Most of the historic places of interest are found in the old section along the picturesque quayside. Wine tastings, offered at the Office of Tourism, feature not only Pouilly-Fuissé but also the famous Beaujolais wines from the vineyards just south of the Mâconnais.

The vast majority of the **Beaujolais** wine district lies below Burgundy in the department of Rhône, but a mere geographical boundary seems no excuse for omitting this wine from our discussion. Actually, the Beaujolais district is bigger than any of the other wine districts, outpro-ducing them all to the tune of 150 million bottles a year, and its northern tip overlaps the southern section of the Mâconnais. When Beaujolais gets to the market, vendors may buy it as Mâcon-Village and sell it as Burgundy thinking that the latter may be better known. A mild climate, idyllic wine villages, and a scenic landscape of rolling hills and valleys all add to the allure of Beaujolais country.

The best-quality wines are grown in the northern part of the district where ten *crus* are clustered around some thirty-nine villages. Red and white Beaujolais are produced from Gamay and Chardonnay grapes. Most Beaujolais wines are best drunk when young. Around the wine-drinking world, of course, the best-known version is Beaujolais Nou-veau, the wine that comes to market on the third Thursday in November and is ready for immediate consumption. The tremendous hoopla associ-ated with this relatively recent phenomenon is one of the great PR triumphs of the wine trade, now representing about one half of all Beaujolais production. Some wine snobs have not joined in this "prole-tarian" movement, and the local wine growers themselves must be bemused to hear profound pronouncements on the merits of each year's harvests from the self-anointed authorities in Paris, London, and New York. Overlooked almost entirely is the fact that there are many very fine fruity and full-bodied Beaujolais produced in the ten *crus* regions mentioned above. But perhaps one should not expect a greater degree of practicality and logic in the wine scene than in other areas such as cuisine or the arts which are so caught up in trends and fashion. Maybe what matters most is that the worldwide popular demand for wine is growing at incredible rates, and for Burgundy that is nothing but good news.

Here we must end our tour of the vineyards of Burgundy. We hope that it will encourage bargers to take advantage of their time in Burgundy to learn about and partake of the great diversity of wines and that other readers already knowledgeable about wines will be tempted to enjoy them while floating along the waterways of France.

List of Charter Companies

Company	Business Address	Business Phone
Abercrombie & Kent International, Inc.	1520 Kensington Road Oak Brook, IL 60523-2141 USA	(800) 323-7308
Alden Yacht Charters	1909 Alden Landing Portsmouth, RI 02871	(401) 683-1782
Bargain Boating/ Morgantown Travel Services	1909 Alden Landing Portsmouth, RI 02871	(800) 662-2628
Barge Broker	2321 30th Street Boulder, CO 80301	(303) 447-3582
Boat Inc., Le	10 South Franklin Turnpike Ste. 204B Ramsey, NJ 07446	(201) 236-2333
European Waterways	140 E. 56th St., #4C New York, NY 10022	(212) 688-9464
France Afloat	1 Quai du Port 89270 Vermenton France	+33 (3) 86-81-67-87
French Country Waterways	P.O. Box 2195 Duxbury, MA 02331	(800) 222-1236
Jody Lexow Yacht Charters	26 Coddington Wharf Newport, RI 02840	(800) 662-2628
KD River Cruises of Europe	2500 Westchester Avenue Suite 113 Purchase, NY 10577	(800) 346-6525
Kemwel Premier Selection	106 Calvert St. Harrison, NY 12603	(800) 234-4000

Company	Business Address	Business Phone
Locaboat Plaisance	Port au Bois BP 150 89303 Joigny, CEDEX France	+33 (3) 86-91-72-72
Lynn Jachney Charters	P.O. Box 302 Marblehead, MA 01945	(800) 223-2050
Papillon Croisière Fluviales de Bourgogne	P.O. Box 2923 Savannah, GA 31401	(800) 642-0577
Springer's Cruises	2305 N.E. Trailway Poulsbo, WA 98370	(206) 697-8594
The Barge Lady	1425 Bayview Avenue, #204 Toronto, ON, Canada M463A9	(800) 880-0071

Source: Eastern France Tourist Board.

APPENDIX C 🍇
Internet Sources

A huge amount of information on France is available through various Internet sources such as AOL Travel File, broken down into the major regions of France where you will find images, videos, and accommodation data.

Useful French government web addresses for general information on tourism include the French Tourist Office at www.francetourism .com (note separate web sites for French Government Tourist Office and Maison de la France) and the Eastern France Tourist Board, with the Regional Committee on Tourism in Burgundy at www.bourgogne-tourisme.com.

A search for barging in Europe also yields a wealth of useful information from many commercial sources covering not only Burgundy but the rest of France and all of Europe. From these sources you can learn about comparative prices for cruises with different companies, specific barges and their routes, places to visit, restaurants along the canals, and even recipes. Many charter companies have their own web sites.

An informative site is at www.burgundy-canal.com. Its pages for the canal include "Where is it?" with a map, "How it works" with an interactive animation showing lock operation upstream and downstream, and "History." It presents three lists of hotel barges—alphabetical, top ten (based on surveys of passengers and crews), and different cruising areas. The surveys used to create the top ten list cover such items as French cooking, wines, cabin size, crew-passenger ratio, and average locks per day. Another chart compares the average costs per person of bare barge charters for both low season and high season. Special pages deal with restaurants and cafés, places to visit, hotels and other lodging, Burgundy cuisine, and a crew search for pilots, deck hands, cooks, and guides.

Barges in France at www.bargesinfrance.com is hosted by a division of Special Places Travel of Annapolis, MD, advertising customized itineraries for would-be bargers or any other travelers in France. It helps plan all kinds of travel from start to finish and solicits email inquiries from prospective clients. It presents a useful comparative chart of barges carrying from four to twenty-four passengers.

Barging through France at www.bargingthroughfrance.com is the site of film producer Richard Goodwin, a barge owner based in London. He offers for sale a series of videos on his experiences in barging throughout France. Special pages cover his recipes and price lists.

Peter Deilmann Cruise Lines has a site on luxury hotel barges in the six major barging regions of France at www.peterdeilmann.com.

The major chefs and their restaurants now have their individual web sites, as, for example, www.bernard-loiseau.com.

APPENDIX D

List of Recipes

Travel Guide Ranking Systems

The number and variety of travel guides for France seem to grow at the same pace as travel itself. This appendix presents some of the most widely used guides. While some guidebook publishers design their products to appeal to broad segments of the traveling public, others aim more specifically toward certain markets. The oldest and best-known guides are those of Michelin, which publishes both the red guides for restaurants and hotels and the green guides for sightseeing and touring. Michelin guides originated 100 years ago, and they began awarding the famous stars to restaurants in 1926 when forty-six *tables régionales* were recognized. The 2000 edition of the red guide, running to 1488 pages, devotes eighteen pages of the introduction to the English-language explanation of the guide and its symbols or icons for ranking establishments. A few highlights of these pages follow:

The Red Michelin

Hotels

The six categories of hotels range from the "Luxury in the traditional style" class to the "Simple comfort" class. The five sizes of hotel icons delineate the first five classes while a little man under a roof designates "Simple comfort." In addition the first five classes have from five to one crossed fork. "Pleasant establishments" receive icons in red instead of black print.

Cuisine

Michelin awards three levels of stars (actually little rosettes) to restaurants:

22 restaurants offering exceptional cuisine worth a special journey receive three stars.

70 restaurants with exceptional cooking and worth a detour receive two stars.

407 restaurants each "Very good in its category" receive one star.

436 restaurants with good food at moderate prices receive the red *Bib Gourmand* icon.

The guide contains maps showing the location of the several classes of restaurants.

The Green Michelin

The green guide awards stars to places to visit. Three stars are "worth a journey"; two stars are "worth a detour"; and one star is "interesting." Separate maps designate "Principal sights," "Touring Programmes," and "Leisure Cruising." The Burgundy guide, to take an example, contains a thirty-three-page introduction on the natural history of the land, its political history, art, architecture, etc. The icons or symbols for places, roads, and physical landmarks are presented on the last page of the introduction.

Relais & Châteaux

This chain of *Relais gourmands,* hotels and inns in some forty countries, recognizes establishments distinguished for their cuisine, ambiance, and service. France, with nearly 140 listings, has more representation in this chain than any other country. Different colored *fleur-de-lis* icons stand for the three categories of establishments. Blue represents "A beautiful establishment with a high level of comfort of the '*relais de campagne*' type." Yellow designates "The refined comfort of a magnificent residence." Purple represents "An exceptional establishment featuring the highest level service, amenities, and furnishings." A red icon of a chef with a *coque* designates a restaurant known for excellent cuisine. Nearly twenty icons designate various special amenities.

The Hachette Guide to France

Published by Pantheon Books of New York, this guidebook incorporates in one volume of over a thousand pages information on sights, hotels, restaurants, and recreation. Organized according to the twenty-eight regions of France, it provides comprehensive coverage between the covers of a single paperback. It has its own ranking systems. Hotels range from one star to four stars with an L designating a luxury hotel.

Restaurants are ranked from one to four diamonds. Another ranking system covers places of interest.

Fodor's

The Fodor Guide to France with color map illustrations covers hotels and restaurants in all categories except for the most inexpensive, driving and walking tours, a vocabulary, menu guide, and other practical information. Fodor's upClose France uses a light touch to bring out some of the lesser-known facts, starting with the basics on France and then in fifteen chapters treating individual areas in greater depth.

Frommer's France

Aimed at budget-minded readers seeking to travel well. Lists about 350 hotels but only about 85 of them cost more than $100 per night. Price ranges listed for the 300 restaurants mentioned.

Let's Go, France

This is one of a series of guides designed for independent travelers on a budget. A general section presents French history, Culture, France Today, French food, Wine, Essentials, Safety/Security, and Health. Eight regional sections present the rewards of travel in the various parts of the country with maps showing location of recommended sites.

The Rough Guide: France

One of another series of guidebooks covering much of the same ground as those listed above. A distinctive feature is a section on getting to France from various points of departure in other parts of the world. A separate guidebook under this imprimatur is *The Rough Guide, French Hotels and Restaurants.*

Lonely Planet, France

The Lonely Planet series presents information for a range of budgets including the low end for students and others seeking low cost travel. This guide contains 143 detailed maps, a language section, regional food glossary, information on how to get around in various parts of France, what to do if you're assaulted, and how to avoid trouble.

APPENDIX F

Hotels and Restaurants

This appendix lists only hotels and restaurants cited in the text. For additional information on other establishments not mentioned in the text, consult the guides listed in Appendix E. Items are listed in the order of their citation in the text.

Auberge de l'Ill (also called Château de l'Ill) at Ostwald near Strasbourg, phone 03 88 66 85 00, FAX 03 88 66 85 49

Grande Chaumière, St-Florentin, phone 03 86 35 15 12, FAX 03 86 35 33 14

Barnabet, Auxerre, phone 03 86 52 26 51, FAX 03 86 51 68 33

Hotel-restaurant de la Rivière, Gurgy, phone 03 86 53 02 50

L'Etape des Gourmets, Châtel-Censoir, phone 03 86 81 05 15

Hostellerie de la Poste, Clamecy, phone 03 86 27 01 55, FAX 03 86 27 05 99

Hôtel-Restaurant du Morvan, Cuzy, phone 03 86 29 82 20

Hôtel La Buissonière, Restaurant "Le Marode," phone 03 86 20 02 13, FAX 03 86 20 13 85

Hostellerie de la Poste, Avallon, phone 033 86 34 16 16 FAX 03 86 34 19 19

L'Espérance, Vézelay à St.-Père, phone 03 86 33 26 15, FAX 03 86 33 26 15

La Côte St.-Jacques, Joigny, phone 03 86 62 09 70, FAX 03 86 91 49 70

Thibert, Dijon, phone 03 80 67 74 64, FAX 03 80 63 87 72

Pré aux Clercs, Dijon, phone 03 80 38 05 05, FAX 03 80 38 16 16

Hôtel de la Poste, Beaune, phone 03 80 22 35 48, FAX 03 80 24 19 71

Bernard Morillon, Beaune, phone 03 80 24 12 06,
  FAX 03 80 22 66 22

Hostellerie de Levernois, Levernois near Beaune,
  phone 03 80 24 73 58, FAX 03 80 22 78 00

La Côte d'Or, Saulieu, phone 03 80 90 53 53, FAX 03 80 64 08 92

Château de Gilly, Vougeot, phone 03 80 62 89 98,
  FAX 03 80 62 82 34

Lameloise, Chagny, phone 03 85 87 65 65, FAX 03 85 87 03 57

Château d'Igé, Igé, phone 03 85 33 33 99, FAX 03 85 33 41 41

BIBLIOGRAPHY

Note: The bibliography is arranged in the order of the chapters of the book. Sources used for each chapter are listed alphabetically by book title.

Chapter 1 Some Glimpses of the Past

The Canals of France, Michel-Paul Simon. Coffee-table book of colored photos, Editions du Chene, Hachete-Livre, 1997

Champagne & Burgundy, Passport's Regional Guides of France, Arthur and Barbara Eperon, 1997

The Companion Guide to Burgundy, Robert Speaight (revised by Francis Pagan), Companion Guides, an imprint of Boydell & Brewer Ltd., 1996

Michelin Tourist Guide (Burgundy–Morvan), The Green Guidebook

Francis in All His Glory, J. Burke Wilkinson, Farrar, Straus & Giroux, 1972

Fortune is a River: Leonardo da Vinci and Niccolo Machiavelli's Magnificent Dream to Change the Course of Florentine History, Roger D. Masters, Plume, Published by the Penguin Group, 1999

Chapter 2 From St-Florentin to Chitry in a Week

Canal Barges & Narrow Boats, Peter L. Smith, Shire Publications; unavailable on Amazon.com

Cruising French Waterways, Hugh McKnight, Sheridan House; list price $35.00, 304 pages paperback. Amazon.com calls it "the leading descriptive guide to the network of rivers and canals of France. Information on history and commercial activity of each area as well as chateaux, historical sites and scenic attractions."

Planning the French Canals: Bureaucracy, Politics, and Enterprise Under the Restoration, Reed G. Geiger, University of Delaware Press; list price $43.50.

The Secret Life of the Seine, Mort Rosenblum, Addison Wesley, paperback, list price $12.00. An entertaining travelogue by a former editor in chief of the *International Herald Tribune* who lives on a launch tethered to the banks of the Seine in Paris.

Through the French Canals, Philip Bristow, Pergamon Press, 8th edition, list price $23.00. A valuable and comprehensive guide illustrated with photographs providing practical information on thirty-nine waterway routes from the English channel to the Mediterranean.

Watersteps Through France to the Camargue by Canal, Bill and Laurel Cooper, Sheridan House, Dobbs Ferry, NY, 1991

Amazon.com lists three additional titles, all out of print: *France, the Quiet Way,* John Liley; *Inland Waterways of France,* E. E. Benest, St. Mammaes–Decize in French; *Through France to the Mediterranean: By Canal to the Sea,* Mike Harper.

Chapter 3 The Cuisines of Burgundy

Champagne & Burgundy, Passport's Regional Guides, Arthur and Barbara Eperon, 1997

France, the Beautiful Cookbook, Text: Gilles Pudlowski, Recipes: the Scotto Sisters, HarperCollins, San Francisco, 1989

La Belle France: The Sophisticated Guide to France, Newsletter, October 1994 and May 1995, Travel Guide, Inc. Charlottesville, Va.

Michelin Red Guide, Hotels and Restaurants, 1999

Relais & Châteaux, Relais Gourmands, 1998

Saveur magazine, special issue on Burgundy, November 1998

The Food of France, Waverly Root, Vintage Books/Random House, New York, 1992

The Food Lover's Guide to France, Patricia Wells, Workman Publishing, 1997

The Wine and Food of Europe: An Illustrated Guide, Marc and Kim Millon, Chartwell Books, Secaucus, NJ, 1982

Appendix A The Wines of Burgundy

Burgundy: Touring in Wine Country; Mitchell Beazley and Hubrecht Duijker, Octopus Publishing Group, London, 1996

Champagne & Burgundy, Passport's Regional Guides, Arthur and Barbara Eperon, 1997

The Food Lover's Guide to France, Patricia Wells, Workman Publishing, New York, 1987

The Food of France, Waverly Root, Vintage Books/Random House, New York, 1992

The Wine and Food of Europe, Marc and Kim Millon, 1982

Wines of France, Alexis Lichine, Cassell & Co. Ltd., London, 1958

INDEX 🍇

Numerals in italics indicate historical information. References in italics indicate historical information where usage is not typical.

A

abbeys
  Benedictine, 4, 6–7
  Cistercian, 4
  Citeaux, 68
  Cluny, 4, 6–7
Agrippan Way, the, 39
Alesia, 1
Aloxe-Corton, 87
Alsace, xiv, xvi
Alsace-Lorraine, xv
Antoinette, Marie, xv
AOL Travel File, 97
appellation system
  in Beaune, 86–87
  in the Côte Chalonnaise, 90
  in the Mâconnais, 91
Armagnacs, the, 9
art, 11
  Dijon Fine Arts Museum, 12–13
  sculpture, 1, 39
Auberge de l'Ill, xvi, 105
Auxerre, xix, 28, *37–39*, 62 map
Avallon, 61

B

barges, 23
  accommodations, 30, 31 figure
  bare v. hotel, ix, xx
  sizes and number of guests accommodated, xxii
  website information, 97
barging
  debris and, 35
  unreliability of marina staff information, 33
  videos on, 98
  See also charter companies; locks

Barnabet, 28, 105
Barnabet, Jean-Luc, 29
Basilica of St. Mary Magdalene, 4
Beaune, xvii–xviii, *11*, 62 map, 66–67, 80 graph
  appellations in, 86–87
  mustard and, 60
  wine auctions, 12
Belle France, La (newsletter), xviii, 28, 64
Benedictines, the, 3, 6–7, 91
Bernard, St., 3, 68
Bernard Morillon, 67, 106
Billoux, Jean-Pierre, 66
Bonvalot (chef), 27
Bordeaux, xvi
  mustard and, 60
Brosse, Claude, 91
Burgundy
  canals and waterways, x map
  departments, 62 map
  geographic diversity of wines, 80 graph
  history, *1–21*
  name of formally abolished, 20
  Regional Committee on Tourism, 97
Burgundy Canal, x map, xix, 62 map

C

canals and waterways, x map
  Burgundy Canal, 25 map
  and construction of, 19–20
  da Vinci and, 14–15, 16
  debris and, 35
  Francis I and, 14–15
  the Freycinet standard, 20
  local fisherman, xxiv

W

Wells, Patricia, 64, 65, 66, 68
wine
  Alsatian, xvi
  appellation system, 82–83
  Beaujolais, 82
  Beaujolais Nouveau, 92
  Chablis, 58, 65, *83–84*
  Chambertin, 85
  Chardonnay, 81
  classes of, 82
  Corton Charlemagne, 87
  geographic diversity of, 80 graph
  Gewurztraminers, xvi
  in the Mâconnais, 90
  Marc de Bourgogne, 55
  Meursault, 88
  Pinot Noir, 81
  Pommard, 87
  Pouilly-Fuissé, 91, 92
  Pouilly-Loché, 92

  Pouilly-Vincelles, 42, 92
  Reislings, xvi
  St. Veran, 92
  La Tâche, 86
  Volnay, 88
  See also grapes; vineyards
wine auctions, 12
wine cellars
  Burgundy Wine Museum, xviii
  Chateau de Meursalt, 88
  Chateau du Passe-Temps, 89
  See also caves
wine sauces, 58
wine tasting, 88
  "Brotherhood of Wine Tasting
    Knights," 68–69
  Office of Tourism, 92

Y

Yonne, 58, 61–65, 62 map
Yonne, the, *19*, *39*, 62 map